NF
712.6
DILL

W9-BBS-585

Trimble Co. Public Library
35 Equity Drive
Bedford, KY 40006

1

The Garden View

The Garden View

Designs for Beautiful Landscapes

Tara Dillard

Trimble Co. Public Library
35 Equity Drive
Bedford, KY 40006

Sterling Publishing Co., Inc.

New York

Prolific Impressions Production Staff:

Editor in Chief: Mickey Baskett
Creative Director: Joel Tressler
Graphics/Photography: Joel Tressler
Illustrations: Shannon Pable, Stephen Henson
Administration: Jim Baskett

Every effort has been made to insure that the information presented is accurate. Since we have no control over physical conditions, individual skills, or chosen tools and products, the publisher disclaims any liability for injuries, losses, untoward results, or any other damages which may result from the use of the information in this book. Thoroughly read the instructions for all products used to complete the projects in this book, paying particular attention to all cautions and warnings shown for that product to ensure their proper and safe use.

No part of this book may be reproduced for commercial purposes in any form without permission by the copyright holder. The written instructions and design patterns in this book are intended for the personal use of the reader and may be reproduced for that purpose only.

Library of Congress Cataloging-in-Publication Data
Dillard, Tara.
The garden view : designs for beautiful landscapes / Tara Dillard.
p. cm.
Includes index.
ISBN 1-4027-1405-X
1. Gardens--Design. 2. Landscape gardening. I. Title.
SB473.D53 2004
712'.6--dc22

2004009112

1 2 3 4 5 6 7 8 9 10

Published by Sterling Publishing Co., Inc.
387 Park Avenue South, New York, N.Y. 10016

© 2005 by Prolific Impressions, Inc.
Produced by Prolific Impressions, Inc.
160 South Candler St., Decatur, GA 30030

Distributed in Canada by Sterling Publishing
c/o Canadian Manda Group, 165 Dufferin Street
Toronto , Ontario, Canada M6K 3H6

Distributed in Great Britain by Chrysalis Books Group PLC,
The Chrysalis Building, Bramley Road, London W10 6SP, England

Distributed in Australia by Capricorn Link (Australia) Pty. Ltd.
P.O. Box 704, Windsor, NSW 2756 Australia

Printed in China
All rights reserved
Sterling ISBN 1-4027-1405-X

— ✍ —

𝒯𝒽𝒶𝓃𝓀 𝒴𝑜𝓊, Margaret Moseley—Kelvin Echols and I were right to fight over you; Penny McHenry—what a dame; Walter Reeves and Gary Peiffer, my first and continuing promoters; Jenny Wolf who is a tireless behind-the-scenes garden doer.

Dana McPhearson & Bill Brown of Little Dixter; Virginia & her dog, Miss Ellie Hendrick—you did it; Harriet Kirkpatrick—your garden is a tale; Lyndy Broder; Karen Klare of the best French garden; Terri Rooks & Jo Anne Hall; Shirley Cole, a garden force; Rosemary & Nick Trigony; Phyllis & Tom Reetz— your garden is a multi-roomed gem; Kelley Dillard; Joel & Ellen Tressler; Lisa & Greg Shortell; Julie & Ric Ford; Gina & Mark Hill; Melanie & Richard Newton; Anne & Andy Sheldon who have a beautiful garden for all the senses; Celine & Wade Stribling; Don & Kay Connelly—self-taught incredible gardeners; Sarah & Matt Miller; Kathy & Tom Trocheck; Audrey Newsome; Diane & Randy Mahaffey; Alice Williams; Paula Refi, a wonder with perennials; Jane Bath whom I'm proud to copy; Debbie Efird who is living a beautiful life.

Anna Davis—you have created a heaven here; Emily Pritchett, queen of the big castle garden; Renee & Denny Hopf with a garden of serenity; Arch Baker—you put my garden in perspective.

If my first garden mentors were still alive they would be well over 100 years old. In memory of Louise Cofer whose garden awakened me; my gardening grandmothers, Bliss Page & Laura Sayers; Mary Kistner whose eyes taught me to see.

TABLE OF CONTENTS

Introduction — 8

My garden view epiphany; How I created my theory of axes and double axes and their relation to garden design

What are Garden Axes? — 10

Axes are views; Axes bond house & garden; Simple line, exuberant plantings; Where are your important axes?

Creating Double Axes — 18

View out & view in; Stunning, difficult axes must be dealt with; Draw, don't shovel

Choosing Focal Points — 32

Trinity; Color; Scale; Mission statement; Art of the bourgeois; Rock rescue

The Pathway View — 38

Woodland path; Pea gravel path; Flagstone path; Turf path; Speak aloud of your garden

A Winter's Garden View — 48

Creating structure and texture; If a garden looks good in winter it will look good the rest of the year

Taking Time for Good Design — 56

Refining and designing; Moving plants and structures

Garden Views into Your Home — 82

Shutters; Lamps on, different bulbs; Back of picture frames; View of couch

Necessities — 96

Camouflaging eyesores; Leading your eye into the garden

Important Rules for Designing Beautiful Garden Views — 106

Views; Double axes; Multiple axes; No axes left undone; House as backdrop; Enfilade

In Closing — 124

Keep refining; Drama leading to focal points; Copy common threads

Index — 126

Metric Conversion Chart — 127

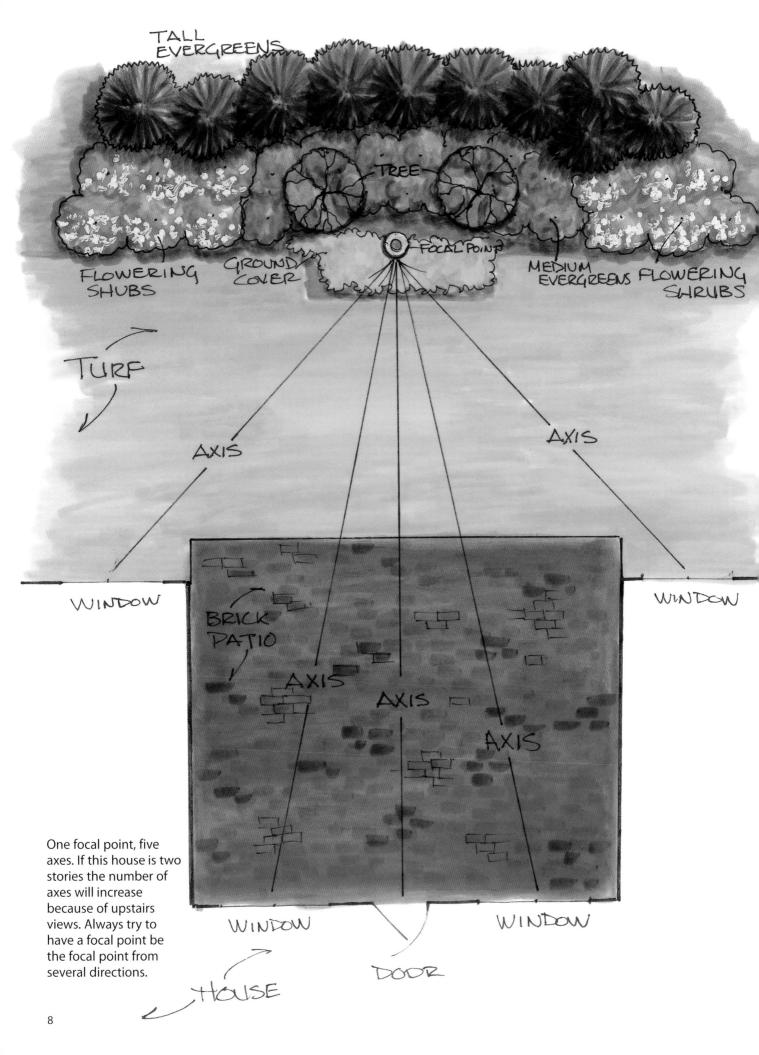

TALL
EVERGREENS

TREE

FOCAL POINT

FLOWERING
SHUBS

GROUND
COVER

MEDIUM
EVERGREENS FLOWERING
SHRUBS

TURF

AXIS

AXIS

WINDOW

WINDOW

BRICK
PATIO

AXIS

AXIS

AXIS

One focal point, five
axes. If this house is two
stories the number of
axes will increase
because of upstairs
views. Always try to
have a focal point be
the focal point from
several directions.

WINDOW

WINDOW

DOOR

HOUSE

My Garden View Epiphany

"In pure architecture, the smallest detail should have a meaning or serve a purpose; and even the construction itself should vary with the material employed, and the designs should be adapted to the material in which they are executed."

A. W. N. Pugin, 1841

It took many years for me to understand that a garden is more than just plants. A garden is a place that offers solitude, peace, and beauty. This beauty comes from plants, yes, but it also comes from where and how we place our plants. This beauty comes also from the artful touches we add to our garden such as beautiful garden benches, sculptures, lovely pots. Both plants and inorganic items we place in our gardens are important focal points. How and where we place these focal points are of immense importance. Our eyes need focal points to bring order to what we see and to guide us along the path of the garden. I feel that the placement of focal points is so important that I have dedicated this entire book to the subject.

There are many, many books available on the subject of gardening. You can learn about the right plants for your garden. You can learn how deep and in what kind of soil to place your plants. You can learn how to build fences and paths in your garden. However, most books do not approach the subject of how to design your garden for optimum viewing of your plants and your garden art. They don't tell you how to create a view that will cause a visitor to want to see more, a view that draws the eye into the garden and leads to the next focal point. I will attempt this task of helping you learn how to design your garden to create a beautiful view.

How I Learned About Focal Points and Axes

One of the best days of my gardening life came at Sissinghurst Castle, England, home and garden of the late Vita Sackville-West. I was in the castle tower photographing views and had an epiphany. A life size statue on a plinth was the terminus (end point) of four major axes. Having toured half the garden, I knew of two major axes. But the tower view had cheated me of discovering that statue's secrets that led me to an axes epiphany. I needed to design the placement of garden focal points to have multiple axes.

College had taught me about focal points and axes—that you place a focal point at the end of each major view (each axis); Sissinghurst taught me another layer of artistic skill—one that increases a garden's complexity yet simplifies its design, one that creates more impact with less input. This is exactly what gardening requires because complexities, even in a beautifully designed and implemented garden, can become a maintenance frustration in just one season.

Axes to a focal point need to also be thought of in reverse, having a focal point at each end of one axis. I call this a "double axis." This concept is now in my toolbox of garden design. The reverse view—usually the house or other building—becomes important. Sissinghurst's life size statue on a plinth, with four axes leading to it, had in its reverse view four focal points, so there were four double axes. Exciting gardens use this tool of garden design.

Not long after visiting Sissinghurst, I came upon the word "koan," meaning "sudden intuitive enlightenment." It was a new word to me and fit what I had been calling "epiphany" and what I had experienced at Sissinghurst. Visit Sissinghurst's garden and think of it as a garden classroom.

Vita's garden at Sissinghurst has more than koan-generating axes. She is also famous for creating one of the first garden rooms of a single color—white. In addition, her yew hedges connect the bits of remaining architecture of her centuries old castle. How wonderful to have your bedroom in one building, the kitchen in another, children in their own building along a path, a library cozy across the garden, and most fabulously, a home office high in the castle's tower that overlooks the garden, orchard, moat and fields beyond. Before Vita's head gardener marched off to war he wrote to her "whatever you do, maintain the hedges."

That single statue at Sissinghurst, seen from the tower, had four axes leading to it. That is not only a low maintenance way to garden, but think of the money saved. With axes angled to the same focal point, only one focal point is needed instead of four.

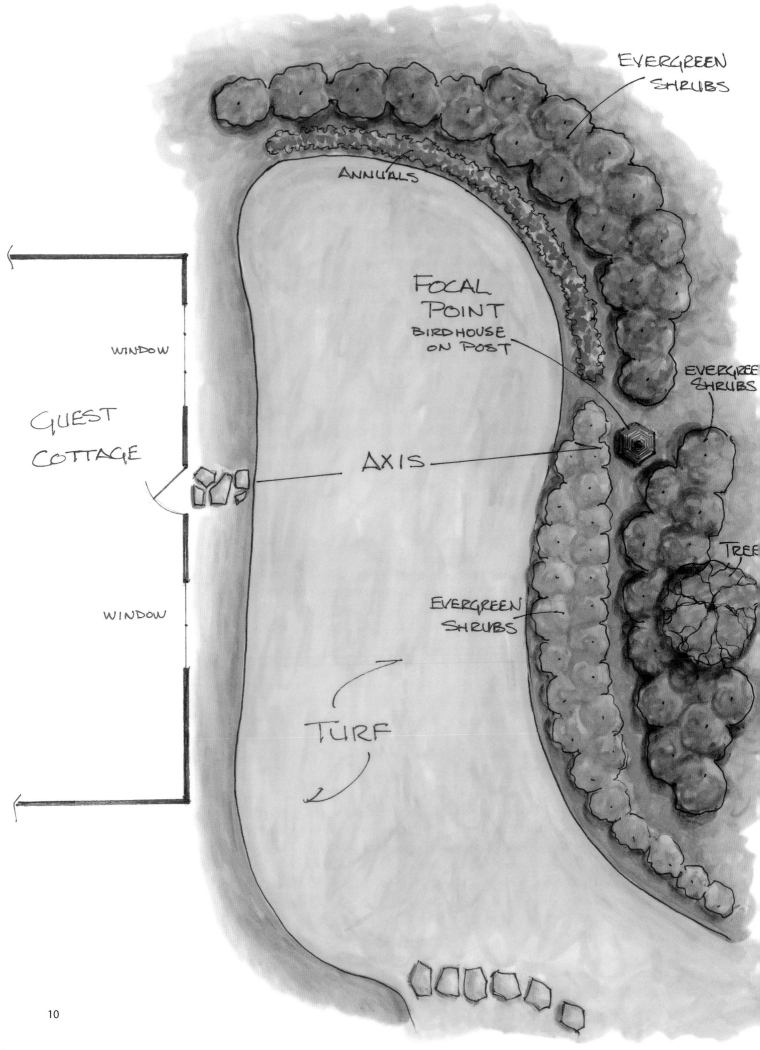

EVERGREEN
SHRUBS

ANNUALS

FOCAL
POINT
BIRDHOUSE
ON POST

EVERGREE
SHRUBS

WINDOW

GUEST
COTTAGE

AXIS

TREE

EVERGREEN
SHRUBS

WINDOW

TURF

What are Garden Axes?

Garden axes are the sight lines (straight lines) that go from your eye to a focal point in your garden. The most important garden axes are those from inside your home out to your garden. In what areas do you spend the most time inside your home? The views from the windows in the kitchen, family room, sunroom, bedroom, office, are your main axes. These are the axes that start your garden design strategy. Place focal points such as benches, birdbaths, statues, and unusual specimen plants where your eye rests at the end of those axes.

When I design gardens I must go into a client's home to see the views to the outside. I must also do some lifestyle "snooping." I try to figure out where clients truly live within their homes and also examine the style of furnishings and bric-a-brac with which they have surrounded themselves. Those two bits of reconnoitering tell me where to put their garden focal points and what style to choose.

Don't Overdo Focal Points

Not every axis requires its own focal point. For each side of your home it is common for many axes to terminate at the same focal point. Your office, bedroom, kitchen, bathroom, and guestroom may all have axes into the backyard. You could place a bench facing those windows that can be seen from all the windows. Result—five axes, but one focal point. I do like to use benches as focal points, even if they will never be sat upon, because of the repose they suggest.

Decide Which View from the House is Most Important

There may be only a few very special elements you would want to plan as focal points. Be sure you place these where they are seen most or seen from the most frequented rooms of the house. A busy single executive had me design his garden. It needed to be low maintenance and provide a great backdrop to the small amount of business entertaining he did. He also wanted a pond. His garden was going to be installed all at once, a significant investment that included night lighting and irrigation. I knew that I must create showy visuals for this amount of expenditure. He had shown real excitement about the garden only when discussing the pond, so I wanted to bring the garden pond into his personal life somehow, yet most days he left home and arrived home in the dark. How could I arrange for him to enjoy it? I milled about the interior of his entire home in some distress. I was finally relieved to see that his bathroom toilet had a large window over it. This provided my answer. His pond was placed on a perfect axis with that upstairs bathroom window so it would be the first thing

"nothing is more the Child of Art than a garden."

Sir Walter Scott

he saw in the morning and the last thing he saw at night. It is still the only garden I've designed with the starting axis being a bathroom window.

Completing garden axes around your home creates the same bond that centuries old Tuscan villas have with their environs. Living in a house bonded with its garden embraces organic living.

DRAWING OPPOSITE: A birdhouse was chosen as a focal point in this garden area. It is placed precisely on straight axis with the door of this guest cottage. What a beautiful view guests will have of the garden. As their eyes sweep along the gentle curves of the annual garden and the evergreen shrubs, the birdhouse can focus their view so that the plants are periphery to the garden art.

ABOVE & OPPOSITE: Both of these photos show the small back garden of a cluster mansion. Cluster mansions are groupings of homes with interior square footage greater than that of the exterior garden. Short on space but long on charm, this tiny garden "lives large." A mix of canopy and understory trees, infusions of flowering shrubs, vines, and decadently tall turf create the illusion of a garden in Normandy instead of what it really is—a new cluster mansion garden with neighbors mere feet away. The same style garden bench is used as a focal point at the end of two different axes. Using the same style bench in both axes makes this small garden appear larger. See the garden plan for this space on the following pages.

SHRUBS

ROSES

BENCH

SHRUBS

ROSES

LOW SHRUB

TALL
SHRUBS

This is for the small back garden shown in the photos on pages 12-13. The garden is a small rectangle of turf edged with a border of mixed shrubs, roses, and perennials. Don't be afraid to use simple lines edged with exuberant plantings. It is a style that goes back centuries and is lasting because of its beauty and ease of maintenance. The benches placed at each end of the garden make the space appear much larger than it is.

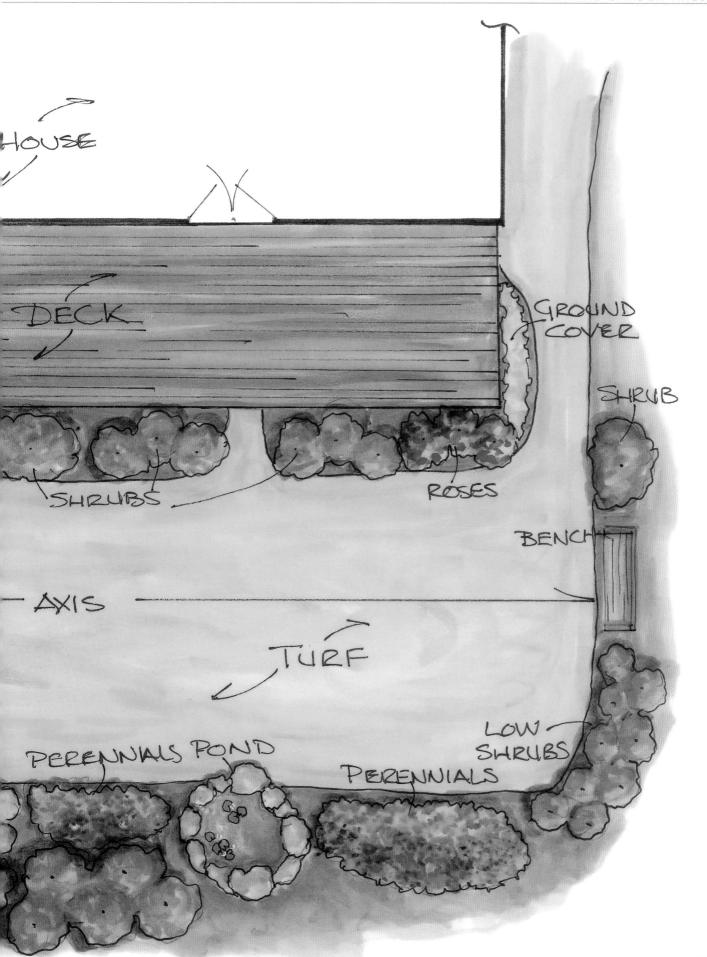

HOUSE

DECK

GROUND COVER

SHRUB

SHRUBS

ROSES

BENCH

AXIS

TURF

LOW SHRUBS

PERENNIALS POND

PERENNIALS

Where are Your Important Axes?

1. Key axes are views from the most used rooms within your home into the garden—bedroom, kitchen, family room, sun room, wherever you spend the most time.

2. If several windows view a common location, place one focal point that can be seen from each axis.

3. Benches as focal points, even if they will never be put to use, suggest repose.

4. Consider night lighting if work takes you away before daylight and brings you home after dark.

5. Completing axes around your home bonds your house and garden.

DRAWING OPPOSITE: An often neglected focal point axis is from the sidewalk of your front door. Many front door sidewalks frame a view straight to the neighbor's garage. However, this axis from a front door path terminates at a focal point, which is also the same focal point on axis with a side window.

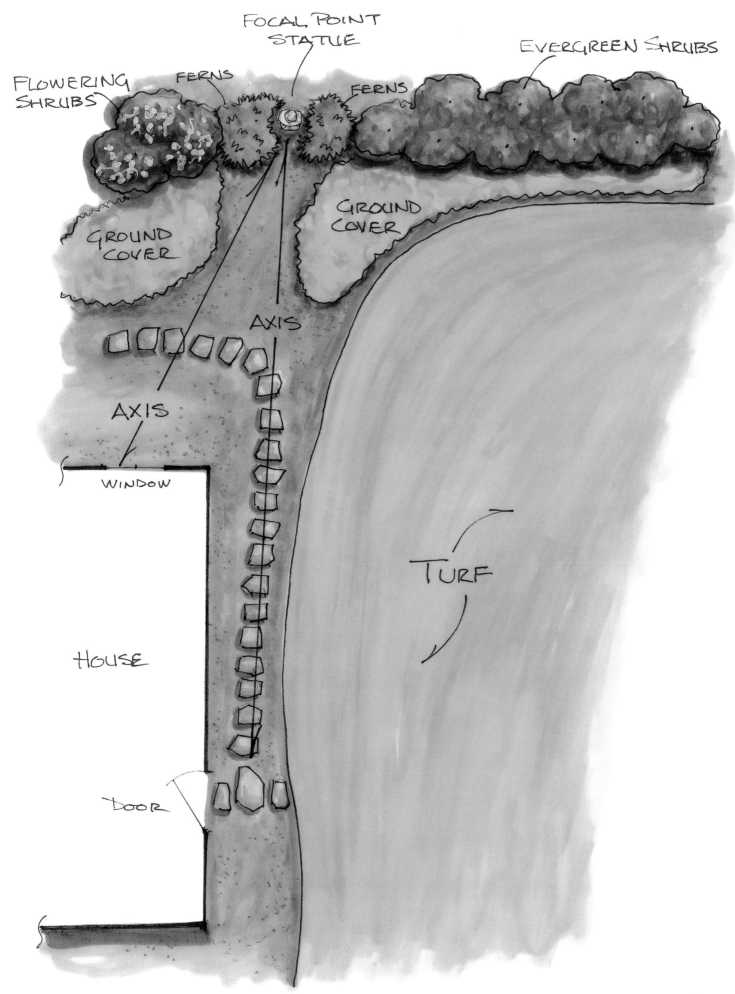

FOCAL POINT
STATUE

FLOWERING
SHRUBS

FERNS

EVERGREEN SHRUBS

FERNS

GROUND
COVER

GROUND
COVER

AXIS

AXIS

WINDOW

TURF

HOUSE

DOOR

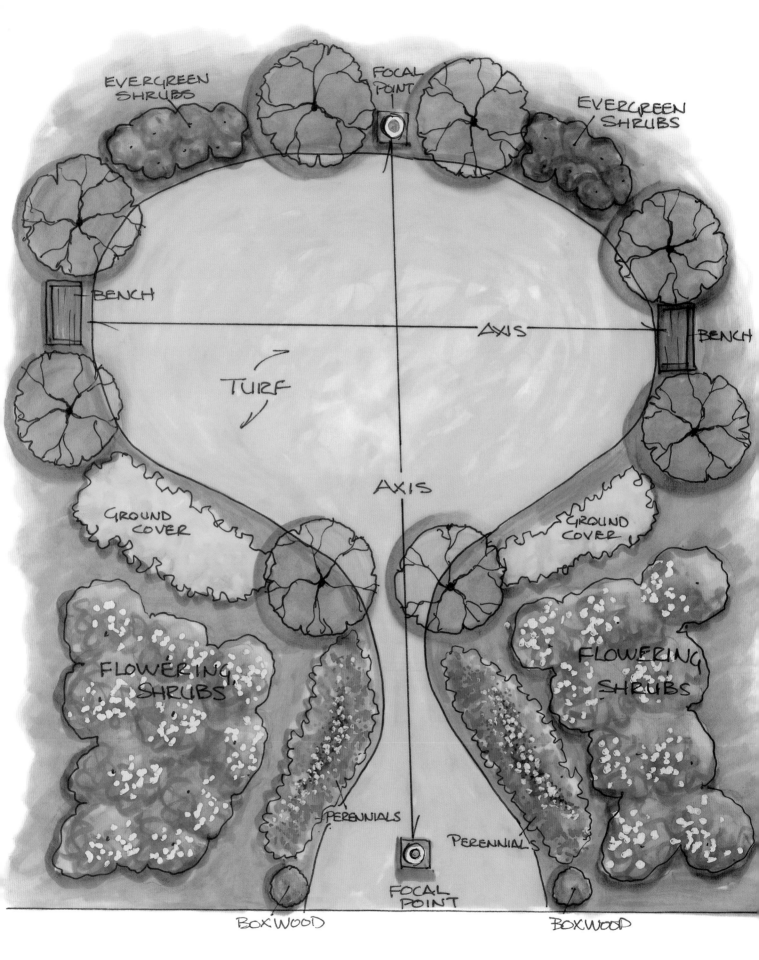

EVERGREEN SHRUBS

FOCAL POINT

EVERGREEN SHRUBS

BENCH

BENCH

TURF

AXIS

AXIS

GROUND COVER

GROUND COVER

FLOWERING SHRUBS

FLOWERING SHRUBS

PERENNIALS

PERENNIALS

FOCAL POINT

BOXWOOD

BOXWOOD

STREET

Creating Double Axes

Gardens align the eye, brain and heart

Double axes are axes about which both ends have been considered—not just the view out to the garden—but the view into the house as well. This is such a simple concept, but not one used in common conversation about garden design. Yet it should be.

Walk through your garden and think, "for every focal point, do I have a double axis?" A focal point bench in the garden on axis with your bedroom window creates a double axis. It's nice to look at the bench from your window, and it should also be nice to look at the window from your bench. If from the bench you are simply looking back at your plain window, the underside of a deck, a door to the basement with a cheap doorknob, and two air-conditioning units, it's displeasing. The axis from the bench must be addressed. Perhaps use shutters at the window and nice interior window treatments, new hardware on the basement door, and evergreen plants hiding the air-conditioning units. Or place the bench at another axis where the view back to the house while sitting on the bench will be pleasing. Instead of a bench as the focal point from your bedroom window, place a lovely birdhouse. Whatever it takes, make the axis view from the bench to the window a stunning one, and vice versa.

DRAWING OPPOSITE: Be bold - have a garden instead of a lawn viewed from the street. This simple garden draws the eye in with a focal point, past a bower of trees, and finally to a far focal point. Surprise awaits inside the garden with a second double axis.

ABOVE & OPPOSITE: This is a maid's quarters from the last century transposed into this century's home office. The owner, an interior decorator, wanted a view to match her interior remodeling. The office window was the starting point for creating a double axes. A picture in an old garden magazine was copied for her parterre. Annuals provide color, or sometimes this gardener skips a season to reflect on the serenity of the boxwood patterns.

CARRIAGE HOUSE / HOME OFFICE

GROUND COVER

BOXWOOD WINDOW BOXWOOD

BENCH

GROUND COVER

SHRUBS

PATH PEA GRAVEL

ANNUALS

AXIS

SHRUBS

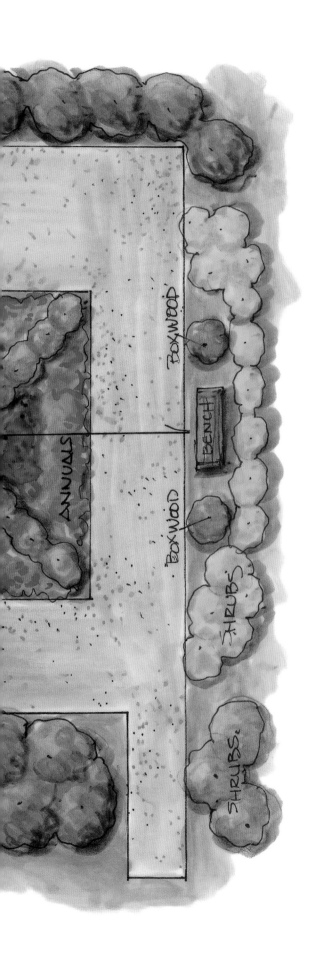

DRAWING LEFT: This drawing is of a parterre garden. The old carriage house was converted into a home office. The placement of the garden was designed from the office window axis. This is a very symmetrical garden style, with benches placed at each end.

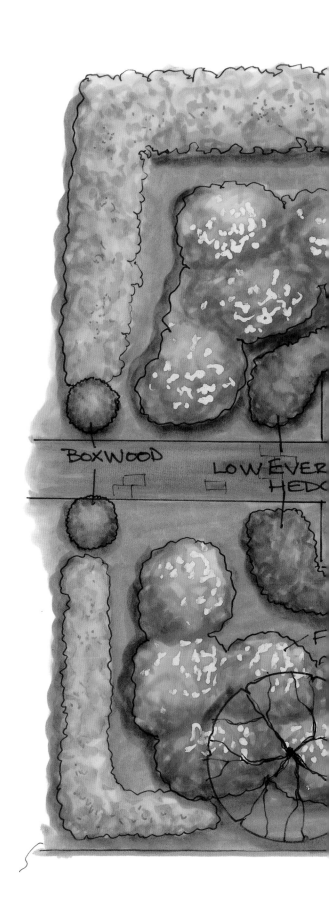

BOXWOOD

LOW EVER
HEDG

ABOVE: This charming garden swing is shown from two different axis views from the house. It is not only a gorgeous focal point, put an anticipated destination. The garden is small, but multiple views of the swing make the garden appear fresh and new from every view.

DRAWING OPPOSITE: This drawing shows an upstairs axis view of a pond garden. Sitting at the pond's edge and looking back at the bench, the garden and house are also an axis view. If you can look out at a good view, you must also be able to look "in" at a good view. This creates what I call a "double axis."

TALL FLOWERING HEDGE

FLOWERING SHRUBS

POND

AXIS

LOW EVERGREEN HEDGE

BOXWOOD

POT

POT

BENCH

RING SHRUBS

AXIS

AXIS

CREPE MYRTLE

CREPE MYRTLE

CREPE MYRTLE

WINDOW

WINDOW

Beautiful double axes should be ubiquitous, off important views from your home. Many views are often not considered. For homes in subdivisions, there are two commonly ignored areas in which to add double axes—the sides of your house. Afterall, many times this is the only view of your house your neighbor may see. How ingenious (and thoughtful) it would be to create a beautiful little garden with a double axis in an area you might think of as only "the air-conditioning side of the house."

In gardens I design, I think of no element in lesser terms than stunning, sublime, graceful. It doesn't matter if the area in question has A/C units, faucets, electric boxes, a dog run, garbage cans, or a compost bin. When finished, all those areas must pass this test question: "Would a photograph of this view be so fabulous it could be on the cover of a garden magazine?" Think that seriously about

every area of your garden. Gardens are important; your environment will either support you or weaken you.

ABOVE: This central window of this house initiated the creation of the beautiful focal point in the photo at right. It is also a double axis. A historic reproduction sundial is on axis with the "arms reaching for joy" statue. Climbing roses on the house add the illusion of more garden than exists. OPPOSITE: Here's a classic enfilade, which is a view through to a view. This "arms reaching for joy" statue is viewed through the rose garden, the fence, past the lawn, and over the pond, and backed by a lush conifer hedge. All this is in a tiny amount of space. It's a young garden that proves that old garden design rules get results. A central window of the family room in the photo at left was the starting point of this axis.

ABOVE: This photo shows the view of the garden through the central window of this home. Viewing your garden from the inside is one of the most rewarding aspects of having created a beautiful garden. DRAWING OPPOSITE: This is the garden plan for the garden shown in the photo to the left as well as the photos on the two previous pages. There are no accidental placements in this small garden. The pond was sited directly off the family room window. Knowing a view must be beautiful in two directions, a sundial is placed on axis with the pond. Good gardens are like good novels—the plot thickens.

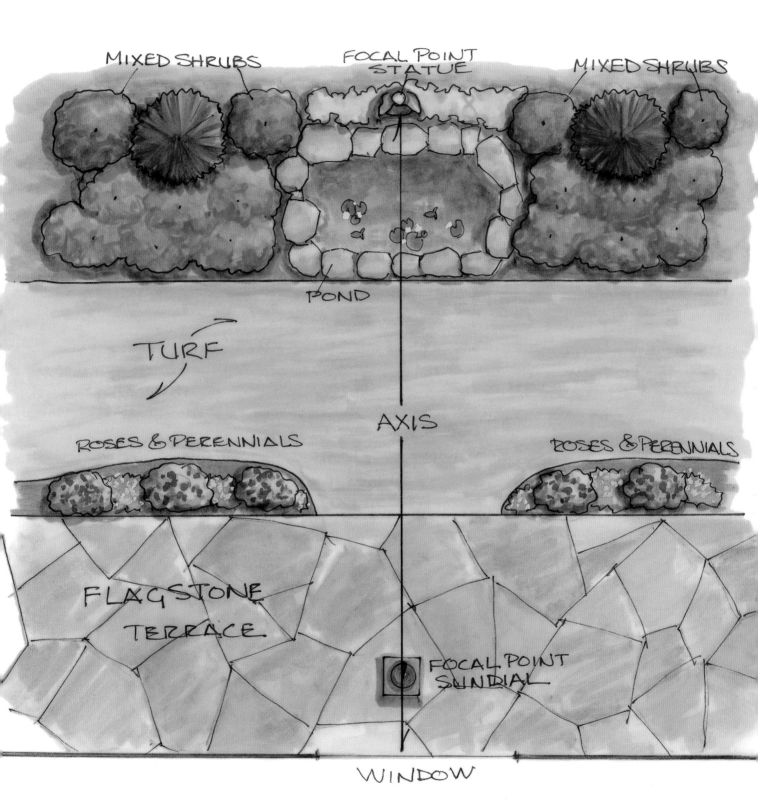

MIXED SHRUBS

FOCAL POINT
STATUE

MIXED SHRUBS

POND

TURF

AXIS

ROSES & PERENNIALS

ROSES & PERENNIALS

FLAGSTONE
TERRACE

FOCAL POINT
SUNDIAL

WINDOW

HOUSE

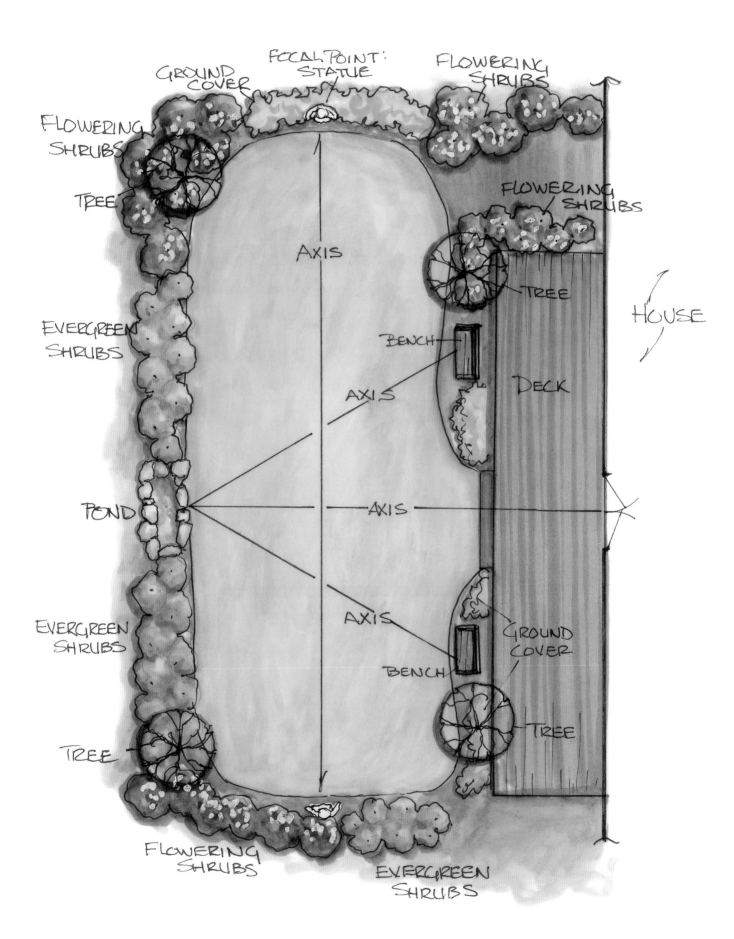

GROUND COVER

FOCAL POINT: STATUE

FLOWERING SHRUBS

FLOWERING SHRUBS

TREE

FLOWERING SHRUBS

AXIS

EVERGREEN SHRUBS

TREE

HOUSE

BENCH

DECK

AXIS

POND

AXIS

EVERGREEN SHRUBS

AXIS

GROUND COVER

BENCH

TREE

TREE

FLOWERING SHRUBS

EVERGREEN SHRUBS

Double Axis Strategies

1. Double axes are the view out and the view in along the same line, each with a focal point.

2. Seeing a bench from your window is pretty.

3. Seeing that window from your bench should also be pretty.

4. Difficult axis views must be dealt with. These include air-conditioning units, faucets, meters, garbage cans, compost bin.

5. Test question, "Would a photograph of this view be so fabulous it could be on the cover of a garden magazine?"

6. All axes should be stunning, with none left undone.

7. Your garden is important. Your environment will either support you or weaken you.

8. The sides of your house are excellent locations in which to add double axes.

9. Double axes should be ubiquitous, off all key views.

DRAWING OPPOSITE: This garden plan shows another small rectangular garden. I often play with garden plans, moving garden furniture, art, and other items around until I fall in love with their placement. It's much easier to play in your garden with drawings instead of shovels and heavy focal points. Draw your garden plan first. Then sit in the space with strings laid out for the axes, bamboo stakes indicating trees, and black plastic pots standing in for focal points before you turn theory into practice.

Choosing Focal Points

Gardens express the essence of our feelings and memories

Every garden needs focal points to lead people around the garden and make the journey a memorable experience. However, not just any focal point is acceptable as the terminus of an axis. Focal points must be considered from several standpoints.

First is the matter of quality. Ask yourself, "Is this focal point so wonderful it will be fought over at my estate sale?" If you're determined to use something that doesn't measure up in quality, perhaps due to sentimental attachment or because it was a gift, grow an evergreen vine on it and disguise what you don't like.

Consider the style of your focal points. Make sure they match the style and feel of your garden. And your garden should match the style you have inside your home. If your garden is casual, then whimsical focal points will work. A formal, symmetrical garden deserves an elegant statue or a classic urn. Create a conscious garden aesthetic. Every effort must be made to make the house and garden seamless. You are creating a trinity: you, your home, and your garden.

Focal points must be placed at the right height. If you have a perfect focal point and it's not the right height, place it on a plinth. A plinth can be an upturned pot or urn, it can be a tree stump, or it can be an elegantly shaped base. The plinth you use should be of the same style as what it is supporting.

Scale is important. Choose focal points that are the right scale for your garden. Scale or size is simply the relationship of the area occupied by one shape to that of another. Remember that garden spaces are usually larger than indoor spaces. Trees, sixty feet tall can tower above your garden room. Think big when choosing a focal point.

Another consideration when choosing your focal point is color. Color is a subtle yet fundamental design element. Color also determines how well your focal point will stand out from its background. Focal points of black or gray are classic because they are subtle colors and will recede. Your focal points shouldn't compete with your flowers.

Don't think every focal point must be a hardscape item. Many plants are focal points. Weeping or contorted plants are focal points all year; others, like Forsythia in bloom, are temporary.

Don't get stuck choosing a focal point for your axes. If you are having a problem deciding, write a mission statement for choosing them. Examples: I want my focal points to be so Star Trek; I want my focal points to be English cottage; I want my focal points to be handmade; I want all my focal points painted cobalt blue. Make decisions about your focal point choice after you have explored everything available to you and what would suit your garden.

If you cannot find the focal point of your imagination, then wait. Too often I've made impatient focal point purchases and regretted them before they were out of the truck. They were wasted money and time.

OPPOSITE: At the end of this gravel path is a bridge that crosses a small stream. It is a bridge of contrasts—formal design with informal materials. It is a focal point to please the eye and lure the feet. The stream it spans is tiny enough to be traversed by a stepping stone, but the bridge adds more impact and drama to the setting. Notice how foliage ties the bridge to its site.

Good gardens are like good novels,
the plot thickens.

Another consideration is budget. Fortify yourself with this fact—the bourgeois spawns most great art. Create focal points from found or rescued items. Carl Jung stated, "This outbreak (of creativity) is a catastrophe only when it is a mass phenomenon, but never in the individual who consciously submits to these higher powers and serves them with all his strength."

I purchased a favorite focal point, Johnny Appleseed, at a steep discount. Made of cast stone reinforced with rebar, he is sitting barefoot. The tip of his large toe was broken off and rebar was staining the cast stone. It was just perfect, instantly aged. I gave an award winning performance when I asked the salesperson for a markdown because of the broken toe. I would have paid more.

At the other end of the double axes that Johnny Appleseed lives on is a granite railroad marker from a defunct line. Found on the side of the road, it was rescued from the county mowers, which were slowly knocking chunks off.

LEFT: Seen from another axes, this bridge is almost hidden—like a surprise. Axes allow for many surprises. Surprise is part of any good garden design.

Focal Point Choices

1. Points to consider: style, scale, quality, color, height.

2. To assess the quality of focal points, ask yourself, "Is this focal point so wonderful it will be fought over at my estate sale?"

3. Combine your home and garden seamlessly. Create a trinity of you, your house, and your garden.

4. Choose a style that fits the style inside your home.

5. If your perfect focal point isn't the correct height, place it on a plinth.

6. Not all focal points are hardscape. Weeping or contorted plants are focal points all year.

7. Wait for the right focal point. An impatient purchase is a waste of time and money.

8. If you're restricted by your garden budget, create focal points from found or rescued items.

9. Consider hiding statues among plantings as surprises in your garden.

10. Everything looks smaller outside. Think big when choosing a focal point.

11. Consider these as focal points—pots of plants, window boxes, gates, trellises, arch ways, pergolas, fountains, seats, sundials, bird baths, statues, ponds, urns, lighting, planting.

ABOVE: This is effective and low maintenance. It's a garden view that is seen from every back window of the home. Choosing the same style planter for both tables increases their impact.

The Pathway View

My garden has only entryways,
I must remember that is true of my life also.

Paths are roads through your garden. Place them where the routes are the most traveled. Often a worn track in the lawn or a trampled patch through a flower bed is the best indicator of where a path should be placed. A path can be used to link garden rooms together, leading the visitor from room to room. At the dead end of a path, there should be a reward such as seating, an arbor, or a view.

There are many types of pathways. When considering what type of path to use, make sure the material you use matches your house in style and substance.

More formal gardens with a flagstone path edged with brick have centuries of history behind them. Even better than a new flagstone path is an old flagstone path dressed with sprouted bird gifts that are allowed to remain.

The crunch of a pea gravel path edged with cobblestones can make a house sound like a home. Nature will plant where she wants in pea gravel; so can you. Expanses of lawn are pathways, too. All can be axes leading to a focal point.

Groundcovers leading to a focal point create an aura that unites the path and the focal point—this creates axis magic. Visiting older gardens taught me about the serendipity of nature's plantings, especially groundcovers on and along pathways. Planned with various groundcovers in a certain order, nature intervenes and makes a tapestry of groundcover art that not even Picasso, the first collage artist, could equal.

Walking about your garden should be an enchantment. Informal woodland paths of woodchips, 2-1/2 feet wide, edged with fallen tree limbs are a classic. A few errant plants that grow will only reinforce the feel of your woodland path.

DRAWING RIGHT: This drawing shows a garden area with a pea gravel path bisecting it. A surprise along the path is a rustic bridge spanning a tiny stream and overlooking a pond. Axes can be used to hide focal points until they become surprises.

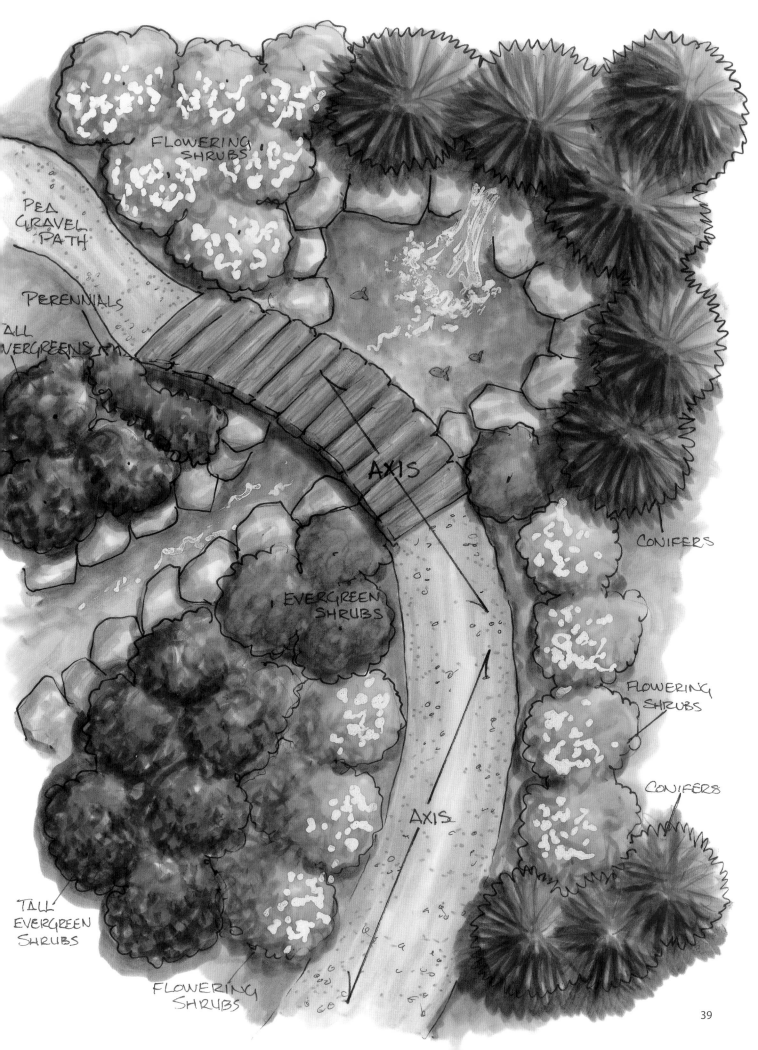

FLOWERING
SHRUBS

PEA
GRAVEL
PATH

PERENNIALS

ALL
EVERGREENS PATH

AXIS

EVERGREEN
SHRUBS

CONIFERS

FLOWERING
SHRUBS

AXIS

CONIFERS

TALL
EVERGREEN
SHRUBS

FLOWERING
SHRUBS

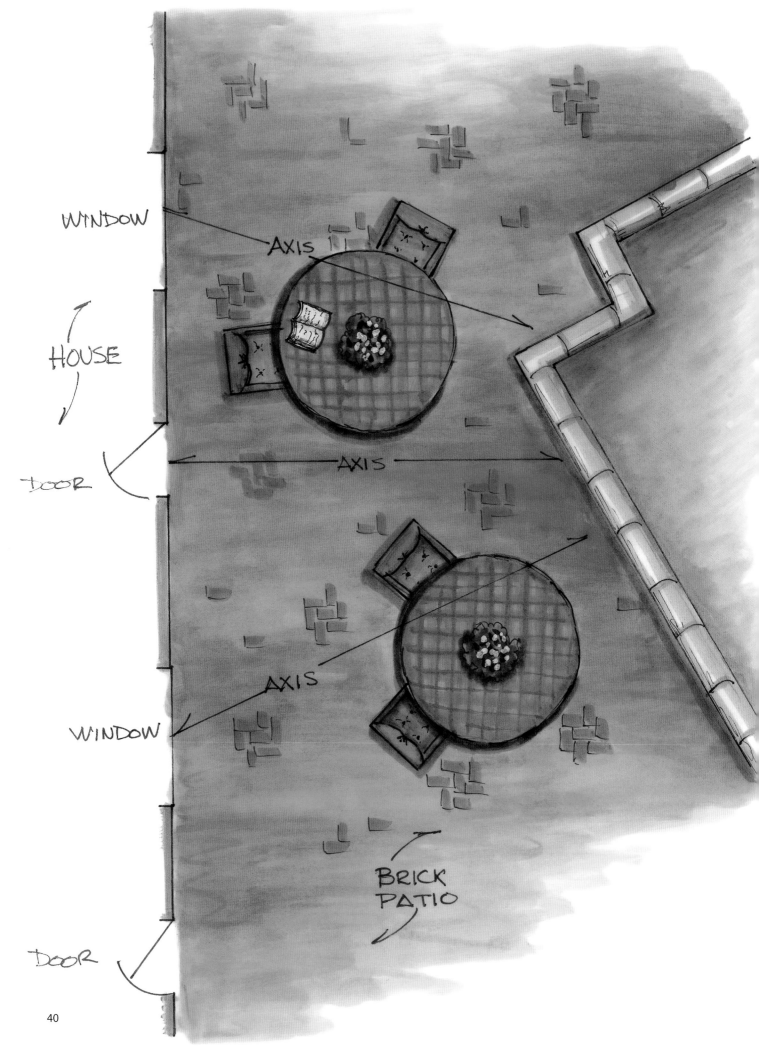

WINDOW

AXIS

HOUSE

DOOR

AXIS

AXIS

WINDOW

DOOR

BRICK
PATIO

*Every effort must be made to make
the house and garden seamless.
You're creating a trinity —
you, your home and your garden.*

Whatever the type of path you choose, make sure it is wide enough for two people to walk side by side. A mistake is often made of making garden walks too narrow. Three feet is wide enough for a hallway in a house but three feet appears very narrow in a garden. One reason for this is scale—we are experiencing the walk in relation to trees which tower over us. A three foot wide path may also seem quite narrow because walks are often encroached upon by plantings. This is the outdoors, allow enough room to move about. The minimum width for a walk crossing a lawn is 4-1/2 feet. If a garden's walk feels comfortable in relation to your body, you are likely to feel comfortable with the garden's proportions. Plants can tower over you or cause you to kneel down for a closer inspection, but you will be experiencing both of them from the walkway.

Children know something about gardens that adults have forgotten. You must be able to get around the entire property. Feng shui specialist, Katharine Deleot says, "You have to let your energy flow." When you can walk around your entire property you've created a magic circle. A few days after hearing Katharine's lecture I purchased a power saw and cut a gate into my side fence. Instead of two dead ends, there are now two entryways. What power resides in words—there's so much energy in the word "entryway" while "dead end" drains energy. Katharine was right. Garden tours no longer get clogged in that location, and when my husband walks his cat on a leash at night, they now include a romp around the garden.

Layers of garden design are like finding art within art, without end. "Each art has its own language," said Kadinsky, Der blaue Reiter.

DRAWING OPPOSITE: A pool and brick patio with two tables are all on axes from every window at the back of this home. The patio is also a pathway. Your garden will improve the more you speak of it aloud with your - gardening friends.

The Pathway View

1. Let nature intervene to create groundcover art in pathways.

2. Groundcover art unites the path and focal point.

3. Walking about your garden should be an enchantment.

4. A few errant plants in your woodland path will reinforce the feel of your woodland.

5. Sprouted bird gifts can improve your flagstone path.

6. Nature will plant where she wants to in a pea gravel path; so can you.

7. If paths are on a slope, consider using steps.

OPPOSITE: You are looking at a close-up within a formal garden. Do not be afraid of the word "formal" when applied to gardening. Most formal lines in a garden make a garden that requires less maintenance. Plants in this formal garden have all been chosen because they are native. Turn the page to see the formal lines created by the plants shown in this close-up.

The Pathway View

8. Expanses of lawn are pathways, too.

9. As children clearly know, you must be able to get around an entire property.

10. Energy should be able to flow freely around your entire garden.

11. Having a path around your entire home creates a magic circle for "chi" - life force.

12. Consider lighting your pathways for night walks in your garden.

13. Paths give your garden direction and rhythm.

14. Surround your paths with lots of flowers and shrubs. This connects your paths to the garden.

RIGHT: This is a formal garden copied from Williamsburg, VA with a twist—it uses native plants only. A circle in the center is on perfect axes within the larger circle and also the arbor and gate. Formal lines and multiple axes make this small garden within a garden quite charming.

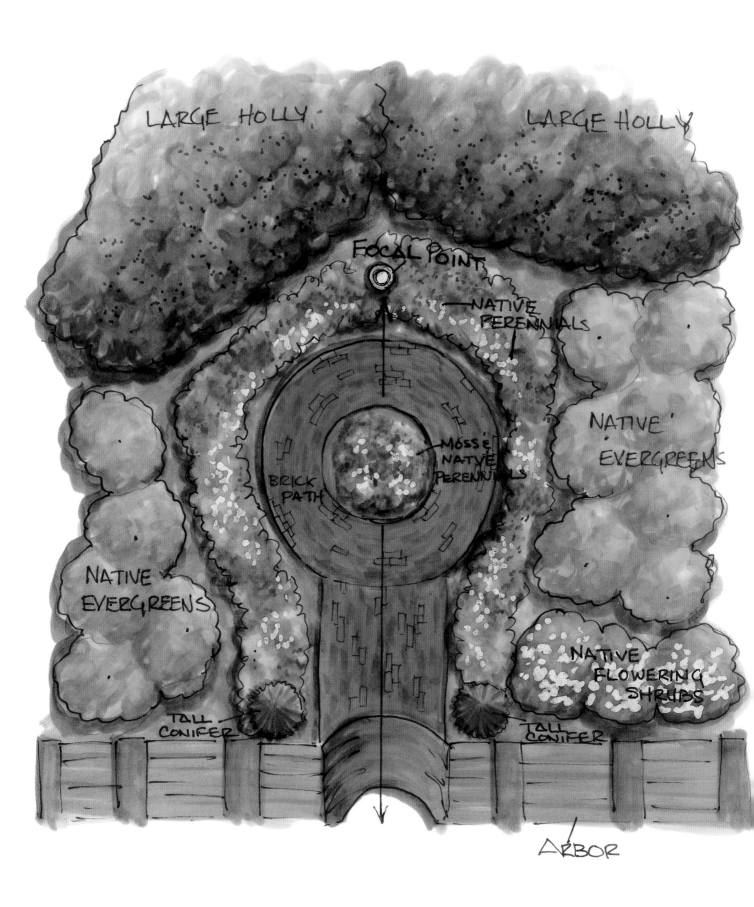

DRAWING OPPOSITE: This garden is formally designed yet informally planted. The whole is formal with its pieces informal.
ABOVE: One approach to formal is using native plants only. This Williamsburg garden is an example. Excitement builds while walking the path and discovering this gate. The garden within is yet to be discovered. From this angle none of the axes are apparent. Lay out your garden to pace discoveries slyly.

A Winter Garden's View

Good garden design will keep your garden view alive and interesting even in the winter. Double axes not only beautify your garden views and streamline garden design strategies, but they also lay the foundation for designing a winter garden.

Add evergreen groundcovers, shrubs and trees along the axes you create. These will be the "floor" and "walls" of your winter garden rooms. If winter is a serious event, axes, focal points, and plantings provide forms to be transfigured into dramtic patterns blanketed by snow.

ABOVE: This axis view takes you down stone steps through a perennial garden, past evergreen turf and into a woodland. Much disappears in the winter, but the structure of the pair of evergreen boxwoods, stone steps, evergreen turf, and silhouettes of trees create a winter scene of strength and beauty. OPPOSITE: Here are the same stone steps as the photo above but from the opposite axis. These two pictures prove that gardens don't have exits, only entryways. Going up these stairs takes you to the deck and driveway. Coming down the stairs takes you into the garden.

My birds may land in the neighbor's trees but they are still my birds.

A garden that looks good in the winter has a great design structure. Elements of line, form, and rhythm have been implemented. The winter garden is not about plants—but it is about design forms. Color, shape and texture are most appreciated in the winter garden. The beauty of summer flowering plantings can often overwhelm a garden's design structure. But stripped of color and blossom, the well-designed garden reveals itself in winter.

Consider contrasts and texture. Tall vertical growing pines next to a horizontal spreading Japanese maple provide contrasts in shape, size, color, and texture. Evergreens as a background for deciduous smaller trees and shrubs can be very dramatic. Some trees and shrubs with interesting shapes include heavenly bamboo, laceleaf maple varieties, weeping aspen and weeping larch.

Color is a consideration that can have dramatic effects. Shrubs with vivid red berries such as winterberry and nandina are beautiful in winter. Other plants with berries to consider are barberry with bright red berries all winter and brilliant fall foliage; hollies that can provide leather-like leaves with deep red to black berries. Plants that offer winter color are Lenten rose (hellebores), witch-hazel, and winter heathers. Unusual hardwoods with unusual bark offer texture in winter. Star magnolia offers shiny silver stems; the weeping delicate branches of the weeping cherry are quite lovely; and birch trees with their dramatic white bark are fabulous.

Another way to create texture and interest in the winter is leave dead plants standing. Don't break off dead heads, or clip and prune in the fall. Dry heads of hydrangea and sedum, tall grasses, stems of daisies—all are beautiful when snow rests on them, creating fantastic shapes and forms.

DRAWING OPPOSITE: Gardens don't have exits, only entryways. This stone stairway from both axes is an entry. Looking up or down the stone steps is pretty and alluring.

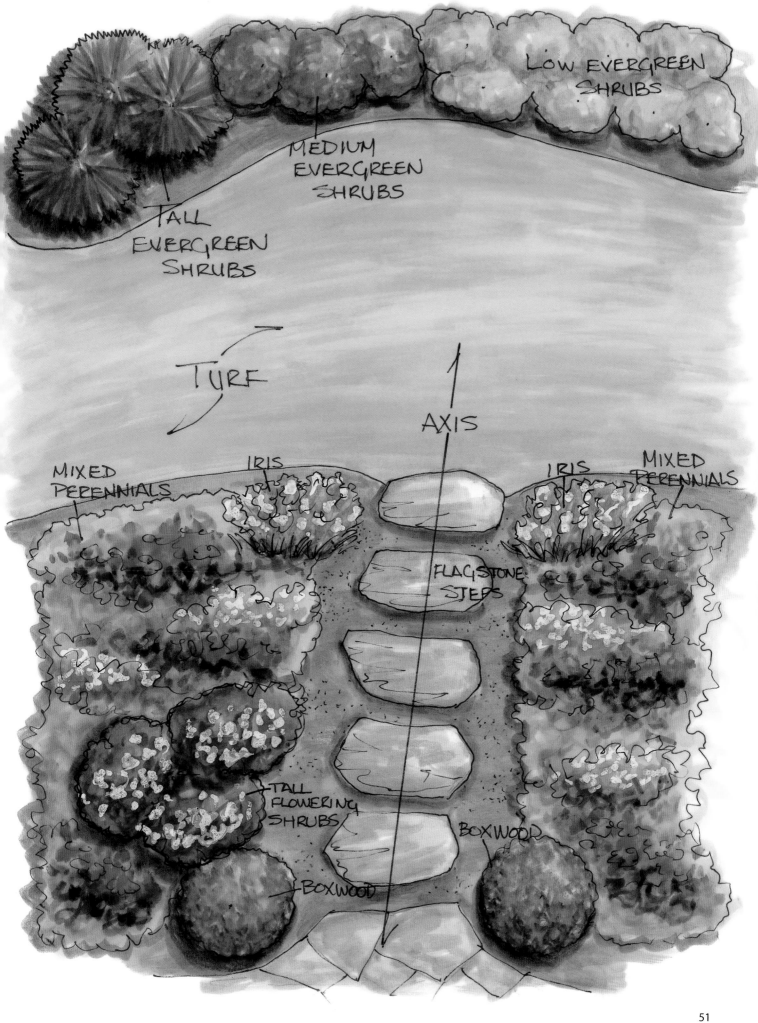

LOW EVERGREEN SHRUBS

MEDIUM EVERGREEN SHRUBS

TALL EVERGREEN SHRUBS

TURF

AXIS

MIXED PERENNIALS

IRIS

IRIS

MIXED PERENNIALS

FLAGSTONE STEPS

TALL FLOWERING SHRUBS

BOXWOOD

BOXWOOD

The Winter Garden

1. Double axes streamline garden design, laying the foundation for your winter garden.

2. Add evergreen groundcovers, shrubs and trees to the axes you create.

3. Evergreens are the "floors and walls" of your winter garden "rooms."

4. Plantings on axes provide forms that will be transfigured into patterns blanketed by snow.

5. A garden designed to look good in winter will look good the rest of the year.

OPPOSITE: Stepping stone squares turned diagonally are exciting in tiny spaces. This path, going from the front to the back of the house, traverses an area 7 feet wide. Beyond that point are dragons and a neighbor's house. The diagonal makes the area appear wider. The many genus of small leafed plants also create the illusion that this small space is much larger. Winter structure here includes evergreens, path, fence with arbor and gate, tree silhouettes, and the house with its many vines.

The Winter Garden

6. The winter garden is not about plants—but it is about form, color, shapes and texture.

7. Ask questions about gardens you like. What will this garden look like in winter? Why is the focal point placed here?

8. Unusual hardwoods with unusual bark offer texture in winter.

9. Design with contrasts and texture in mind to create an interesting winter garden.

10. "The important thing is not to stop questioning." A. Einstein

OPPOSITE: This is the same path but a different axis as in the photo on the previous page. The narrow path, leading from back to front of house, has just as much interest. The area is small. Small leafed plants create the illusion of more space, as does the scale of the child's bench. Another focal point on this axis is temporary—the color of the Japanese maple. Winter interest is held with the structure of the fence, arbor, gate, stone path, evergreen plants, and the child's bench becoming more prominent with the loss of Japanese maple foliage. ABOVE: This axis is to the right of the photo on page 53. No axis was left undone in this small area between the columns is the front door.

Take Time for Good Design

> *If it's good in another garden*
> *it will be good in your garden.*

Don't think that now that you know about double axes and multiple axes with a single focal point you will have it all done by next season or next year. I've noticed that the gardeners whose gardens do have stunning double axes everywhere have long ago retired from a day job. Having a beautiful axis in just one direction is fully acceptable if you have a day job. My own double axes are about 80% complete; the single axes have been 100% complete for awhile. I've been in my home since 1986 and I have a day job. Gardens require time, love, and devotion.

OPPOSITE: Don't know where to start with axes? Start with the architecture of your home. This tiny garden is on perfect axis with the window. Placement of the bench sealed the fate of creating an axis to the window while the watering can, large pot with hydrangea, and window box with boxwoods and ivy all style the axis view. Tapered boxwoods, shown at left, always add emphasis. This is a small area that is part of a larger area with multiple axes—a garden within gardens.

Layers of garden design are like finding art within art, without end.

RIGHT: This layout is a good one to copy in your garden. It has worked across the globe in many zones for over a century; yet it looks fresh each time it's recapitulated. It includes curving turf, nice edging, canopy and understory trees, drifts of flowering shrubs, a few annuals, and a birdhouse on a post placed to be seen from several axes. It's not only a good garden view but you get to enjoy the birds, too.

*Spring
is in
winter's
iciest
garden.*

    I must include the aspect of time in the creation of your double axes because every action of implementing your garden through the years should be a pleasure. When my garden is open for tours, it is fluffed and puffed intensely so you won't realize I'm not quite finished. For most avid gardeners, a garden is *never* quite finished. There is always plants to move around, new plants to try, replacement of plants that aren't thriving in their spot, views and axes to consider.

LEFT: There are a lot of places for the foot and eye to travel in this garden. This is the same garden as pictured on page 57. Well hidden is the bench seen in the photo on page 57. Here it is hiding to the left of the cart. This stone path has a lot to accomplish, leading you to a carriage house, main house, raised terrace, and other parts of the garden.

Do not be afraid of the word formal when applied to gardening. Most formal lines in a garden make a garden less maintenance.

It has been interesting touring gardens in Europe and realizing that many were inherited from a parent that gardened. Some gardens have been in the same family for centuries. Need I repeat, great gardens take time.

Most of the old gardens that I so love to view and garner inspiration from are formal in design. These formal lines help to create a balance and structure to a garden that is attractive to the eye. The formal lines also make it easy to maintain the garden design. You will know exactly where to plant and how many to plant. You can't plant just one. Planting one boxwood means you have to plant another in a facing (or symmetrical) area. Mirror images, symmetrical, simple lines define a formal garden.

ABOVE: From this axis a birdbath and a birdhouse are focal points. OPPOSITE: This old cart has been arrayed in a charming manner to create a nostalgic focal point for this small area beside the house.

*Sometimes, not often,
more is less.*

Not completing every area of your garden will immediately improve the original plan. You have no way of knowing how your plants will grow, flourish, and show off. Several years may pass and your plants may change your mind about not only unfinished garden areas and but even finished areas. Listen to them.

Touring gardens is a great way to help you refine your garden. When you're smitten with a garden you see, ask yourself these questions:

- Why is the focal point placed here?

- Is it just the focal point I like or the focal point along with its backdrop hedge?

- How functional is this garden?

- Is it easy to get to the garbage cans?

- Where are the garden tools stored?

- How can I copy that area into my garden?

- What kind of maintenance does this garden require?

- How much hired help does this garden need?

- How long did it take to create this garden?

- Was this garden professionally designed or created by the owner?

- How will this garden look in winter?

Albert Einstein said, "The important thing is not to stop questioning."

OPPOSITE: The same garden as the previous three pictures is viewed from yet another axis. Boxwoods in pairs prevent this area from becoming visual chaos. They are creating garden "rooms" from the multiple areas that unite the main house and carriage house.

*My neighbor's cat taught me
not to name my goldfish.*

As a child, I was teased by being called "Tara the terror." Now clients and students say I get paid to "Tara'ize" their gardens and lives. It has taken a degree in horticulture, designing and planting my own garden for over 20 years and visiting gardens in many foreign countries to realize what it takes to create a beautiful garden—especially to create a beautiful garden with the constraints of low maintenance and a bourgeois budget.

Knowledge of garden design is not difficult, there is just a lot of it. Much of it is so simple that it's sometimes disregarded, thought of as too silly to do. I know I did that, initially. The topic of this book is just one element of garden design, axes—the views of your garden. Most of you will be thinking (temporarily, I hope), "I'm not going to do all that." Take any new information you gain here about axes, add it to what you already know, then look at your own garden with new eyes. It will take a lot of looking...a joyful lifetime to be exact.

OPPOSITE: You are looking at a tiny, old, in-town front yard. The house is to the left, sidewalk and street to the right. The driveway is in the foreground, neighbor's driveway in the background. This is the entry to the front door—a hedge prevents you from entering from the sidewalk. Plantings are on axes with this summer view. In winter a table and chairs become visible after perennials have gone dormant. It's a postage stamp garden but its own world. This front door opens onto a garden not a busy city neighborhood street.

What will my garden look like in winter?

My garden is my solace. When efforts or events in other arenas of my life disappoint, I'm off to work in the garden. There I find a peace that completely absorbs disappointment, rights ruffled feathers, and lets me fly again. I may be changed but I'm joyful.

Let yourself go and fully create the garden of your imagination. The more you are driven by your garden passions, whether following garden design rules or breaking them bodaciously, the more you are creating a zone of grace. It's "a free gift of providence to man for his regeneration," Webster said about your home. I feel like my home, built on a tiny bare lot, was sucked up by a tornado going to Oz and deposited in a fantastical garden of magical powers.

Gardens speak a language, gardenese. I need joy, beauty, serenity, and grace - all things that can't be bought. Gardens give them freely.

RIGHT: This photo shows a path leading the garden guest from the main house, past a carriage house. There are many plantings of hydrangeas and boxwoods in this garden, adding repetition of form and color. Repetition is an important element of good garden design. Some of the plantings are in pots, adding a break in the repetition. The main house and carriage house are separated by this path, but the area feels large because of its axes, focal points, and creation of garden "rooms." Sometimes, not often, more is less.

Garden Views Take Time to Create

1. Single axis design work is an accomplishment if you have a day job.

2. Even single axis design work for your garden takes years.

3. Double axes design work is more possible if you are retired.

4. Double axes design work can take decades.

5. Many beautiful European gardens have been in the same family for centuries.

6. Not completing every area of your garden immediately, will improve your garden.

7. Plants grow, flourish, and show off, and sometimes cause you to change your mind about both unfinished and finished garden areas.

LEFT: This shows a view up the back stairs to the same main house seen in the previous picture. With so many paths, it could be more like a depot than a backdoor garden. But multiple axes, focal points, repetition, and garden rooms combine to make this a garden, not a depot.

If you want to copy garden ideas, be sure to analyze the entire setting, not just the things that initially caught your attention.

Don't be afraid to move and redesign your garden from time to time to create the views you desire. After my initial "axes epiphany," I knew that I must move a flagstone path so I could create a double axis. As a bonus, it would become an enfilade. The vision of so much improvement pushed me past the inconveniences of moving a path and acquiring another focal point. This is the double axis with Johnny Appleseed at one end and the old granite railroad marker at the other. Between those focal points are flagstone paths, a flagstone terrace with arbor and vines, pairs of boxwoods, a pond, a bench, two pairs of urns and, of course, plenty of flowering shrubs, trees, and perennials. Not only is this the portion of my garden in which to tarry and enjoy for awhile, but it is on axes with every window on one side of my house. Birds, squirrels, fish, frogs, butterflies, praying mantis, rabbits, and a neighbor's cat are testament to how welcoming this garden is.

RIGHT: This is the opposite axis of the previous garden—a hint of the soon to be seen table and chairs. The front door is to the right. Notice how close the neighbor's home is. It's an example of a small garden living huge. With lush plantings, multiple axes, a fountain, birds, and butterflies, this is an exciting space with a lot of movement and change through the seasons.

When recreating a garden you find desirable, you must understand all its elements.

Garden mentor, Margaret Moseley, told me that she sometimes gets up at four a.m., turns on the floodlights to her garden, and just sits and looks for hours. Her garden is beautiful. Close to her ninth decade, she still studies her garden by floodlight then takes action when daylight arrives. She doesn't hesitate to move a mature hydrangea, a stone path, or an island bed. She knows that it takes what it takes.

RIGHT: Here's a beautiful garden view. Much of what you see will disappear in winter but the birdfeeder, arbor, tree silhouettes, and a few evergreen plantings will anchor this area. The birdfeeder is a multi-anchor because of its multiple axes duties. See next page.

ABOVE: Same birdfeeder from previous page is seen on a different axis. This view is from the back garden. There is a front garden view and a back garden view.

What Does It Take To Have Successfully Designed Garden Axes?

1. Placement of garden focal points off key views from the interior of your home.

2. Multiple axes to the same focal point.

3. Multiple axes must be hidden from each other.

4. Garden axes must be designed to be stunning. Anything less is not good garden design.

5. A garden axis should be stunning from both directions - a double axis.

6. Axes views into your windows from the garden must be warm and inviting.

OPPOSITE & ABOVE: Many axes lead to this outdoor fireplace focal point. Usually pictures like these won't go into a book because they are not lush with plantings. It's important to see good gardens before they become good. You will be living with the same situation while you're creating your own garden axes. There are no "after" photos of this garden, but I want you to imagine it fully grown and lush, because that is what you'll be doing in your own garden.

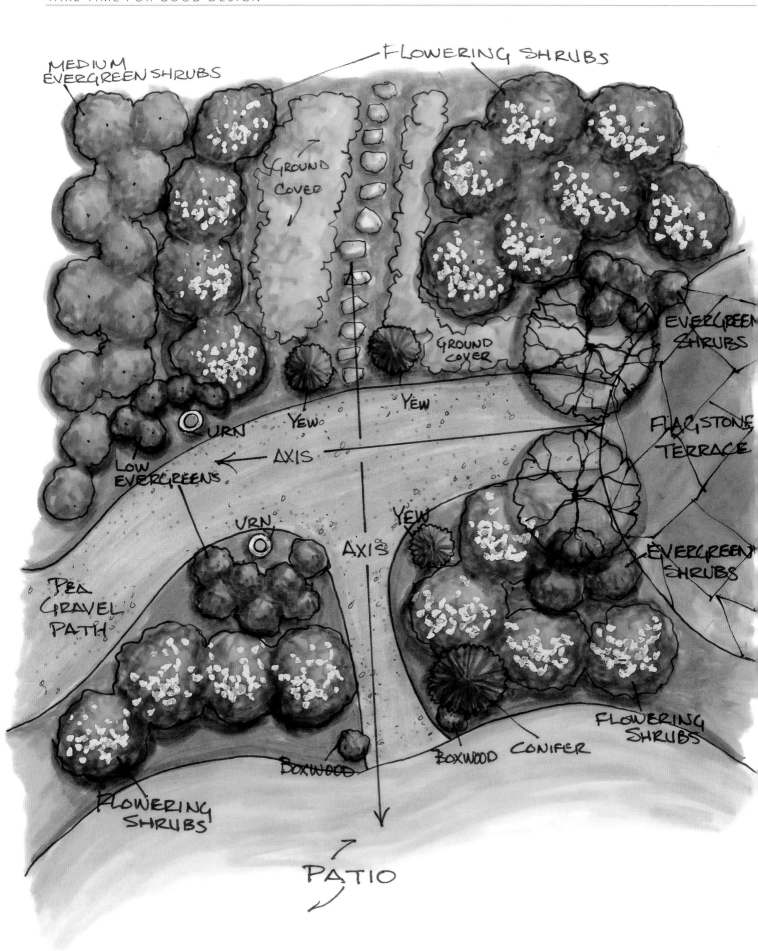

MEDIUM EVERGREEN SHRUBS

FLOWERING SHRUBS

GROUND COVER

GROUND COVER

EVERGREEN SHRUBS

FLAGSTONE TERRACE

YEW

YEW

URN

YEW

LOW EVERGREENS

AXIS

URN

AXIS

YEW

EVERGREEN SHRUBS

PEA GRAVEL PATH

BOXWOOD

BOXWOOD CONIFER

FLOWERING SHRUBS

FLOWERING SHRUBS

PATIO

What Does It Take To Have Successfully Designed Garden Axes?

7. Question for each axis created: "Is this so beautiful it could be on the cover of a garden magazine?"

8. Reconnoiter your interior style to make sure it flows well into the garden.

9. Each garden is different even using the same design rules.

10. Do what your garden demands.

11. It takes what it takes.

12. Time.

DRAWING OPPOSITE: A lot is happening in this little back garden. Using axes to create multiple entryways to different areas has controlled potential chaos. Pairs of trees, boxwood, yew, and urns announce each new garden "room." The area is irregular in shape. Garden designer Sir Roy Strong said in a lecture that the best way to control an irregularly shaped space is to put in a symmetrical geometric shape. Axes have provided the geometry here.

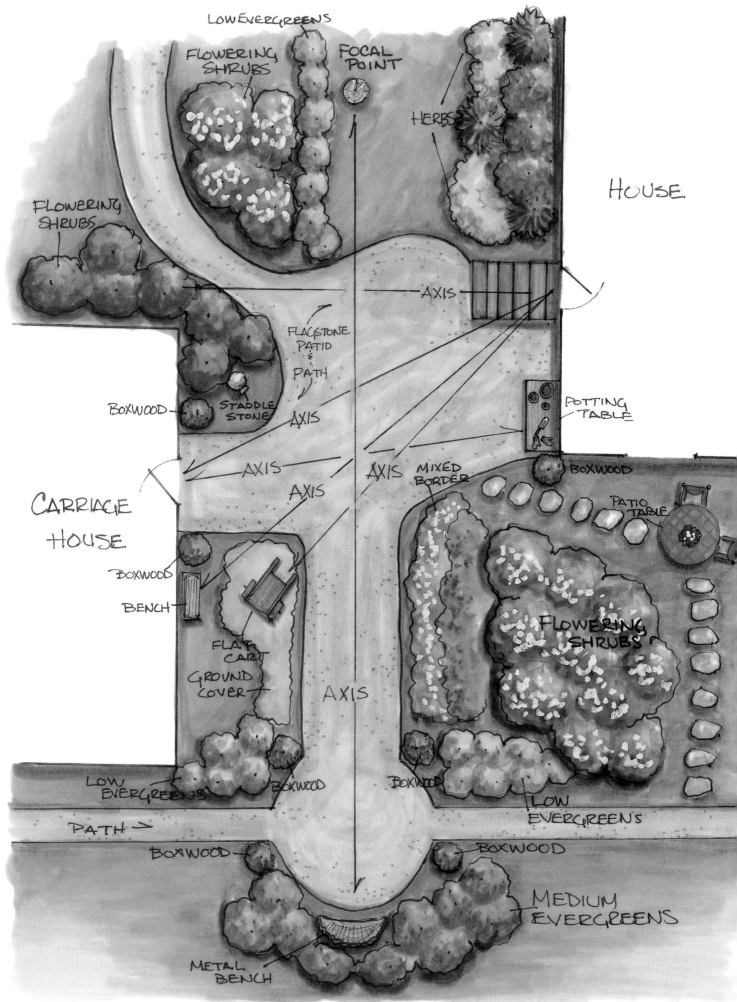

LOW EVERGREENS

FLOWERING SHRUBS

FOCAL POINT

HERBS

HOUSE

FLOWERING SHRUBS

AXIS

FLAGSTONE PATIO & PATH

POTTING TABLE

BOXWOOD

AXIS

STADDLE STONE

AXIS

AXIS

AXIS

MIXED BORDER

PATIO TABLE

CARRIAGE HOUSE

AXIS

BOXWOOD

BOXWOOD

BENCH

FLAT CART

FLOWERING SHRUBS

GROUND COVER

AXIS

LOW EVERGREENS

BOXWOOD

BOXWOOD

LOW EVERGREENS

PATH →

BOXWOOD

BOXWOOD

MEDIUM EVERGREENS

METAL BENCH

Garden Views Into Your Home

> *Always try to have
> a focal point be a focal point
> from several directions.*

Views from the garden to your home should be considered just as intently as viewing your garden from your home. Views on axes into your home should be warm and inviting.

Here are some ideas for making the views into your house better.

1. If the back of your couch is in a window, add a sofatable behind it and accessorize so that it's pretty both inside and from outside looking in.

2. Not enough space for a table? Drape a colorful throw blanket with interesting trim over the back of the couch.

3. Most axes from the garden behind your home, looking into your home, could be improved by adding shutters. Builders are notorious for placing shutters on the front of the house but not the sides and back. Consider adding shutters if this is correct for the architectural style of your home.

4. Don't allow backs of picture frames inside a window to show from the outside.

5. Place that giant TV screen in an area that won't be seen from the outside. I consider this one of the worst offenders.

DRAWING OPPOSITE: This garden plan looks busy and complicated, but it works. There are single and double axes, interesting pathways, and beautiful focal points. The plantings are very repetitious, giving the eye rest and creating a feeling of order and serenity.

Gardens are intimate realms in a public sphere.

OPPOSITE: A passion for hydrangeas and three decades of living in this home have created beautiful axes to the front door. These force you to walk through decadent beauty to ring the doorbell.

> *When creating axes, check their quality by how good they look from multiple directions.*

Consider the importance of lighting inside your home. Interior lamps near windows, turned on, add warmth to a garden. Lamps arrive in my house the way plants do in the garden—it's another fetish of mine. I use a mix of pink and white bulbs in them and 15, 40 or 60 watts mixed about. My neighbor of 14 years told me she noticed how "warm and cozy" my house looked with the lights on. It's another example of going inward toward what we love and outwardly connecting.

When I am designing a garden for a client, I try to take note of the axis from the garden to the house. Recently, when working in a small courtyard with a formal water garden, master brickwork, and a custom table, it didn't leave me much to do or change. The garden already had good structure. However, the view into the house through a large window exposed the back of a long antique buffet and the wires of two lamps sitting on it. The solution was to have a furniture maker craft a beautiful back to the buffet that would also hide the wires. Little things can make a big difference.

OPPOSITE: Here's another axis, from the front door to the street, of the previous garden. There is no backside to this garden, only two fronts. When creating axes, check their quality by how good they look from multiple directions.

Axes views out of my home and into my home have all been designed—out of and into, in that order. When life presents a choice between house and garden, I've already made my commitment to the garden. The interiors and outside walls of my home have evolved to become backdrops which support my garden. It's pure theater—life is the drama. All my windows have a view because I've designed them as still life vignettes. When working in my favorite refuge, the garden, surrounded by lush foliage, blooms, and wildlife, the house seems like an ocean liner in the background—another refuge. You must have areas of your garden that are designed to be sat in during an evening so you can look back at your home, with all its curtains open and the lights on, waiting for Morpheus to take you through another night.

My interior decoration skills have segued from garden to house. I have been able to use many of my gardening tricks in my home decorating. One particular afternoon became quite a rocky ride for my interior lamps. Plinths (raised bases) had been discovered to be incredibly useful and of great impact in my garden. Somehow I made the connection between a plinth raising up one of my pots to using a plinth to raise my lamps—lamps on books, lamps on small antique boxes, lamps on black Chinese platforms.

OPPOSITE: On axes with views from the kitchen and breakfast room, this garden room almost created itself. Originally the birdfeeder was on these axes, but an impulse purchase at the antique market brought home this table and the chairs. A carpet of brick and stone, stacked for years on the site, was woven and the garden room appeared.

"Educating the mind without educating the soul is no education at all….."

Aristotle

Candace Wheeler, thought to be the first female interior decorator in the 1870's, believed "Who creates a Home, creates a potent spirit which in turn doth fashion him that fashioned." Every effort expended in my garden has paid dividends that make those efforts seem small. My garden is an extension of my home. And when in the garden, my home becomes an extension of my garden.

TOP & ABOVE: This woodland swing is seen from front and back axes. Just because a garden is a woodland doesn't mean that axes rules do not apply.

ABOVE: Shown here is a tiny garden with multiple axes. The garden axes do their job of keeping the garden surprising, functional, interesting, and beautiful so that the garden looks different from any vantage point. The house, viewed from the garden is very much a part of the garden. The French doors are at ground level, and when open, the transition from home to garden is seamless.

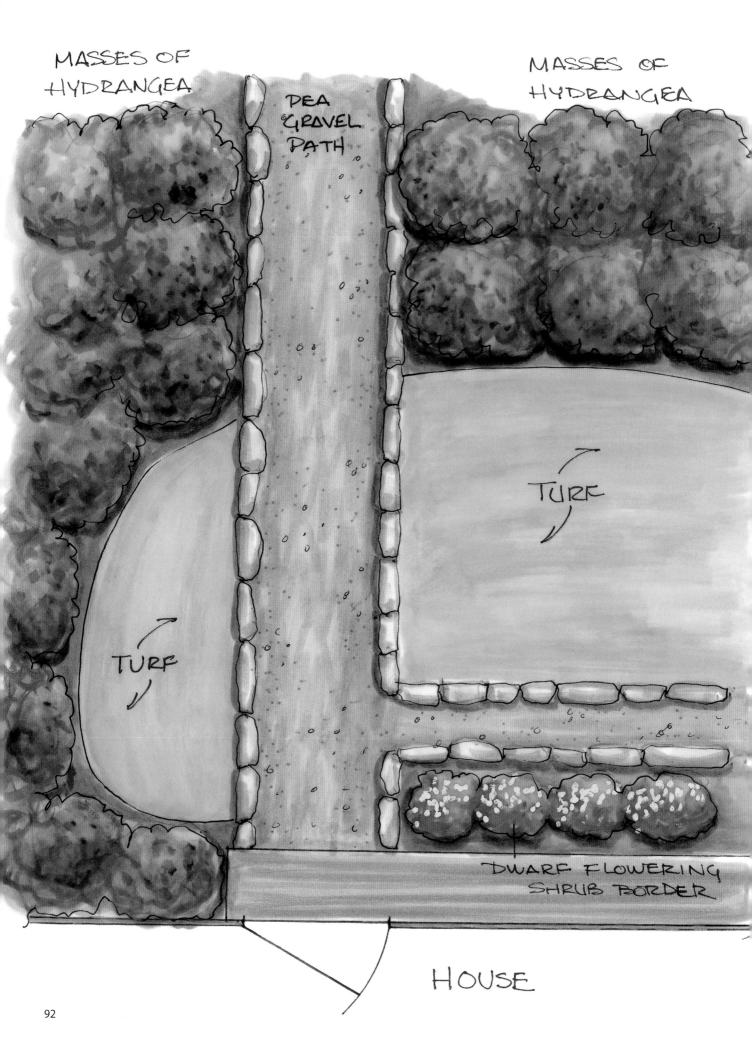

MASSES OF HYDRANGEA

PEA GRAVEL PATH

MASSES OF HYDRANGEA

TURF

TURF

DWARF FLOWERING SHRUB BORDER

HOUSE

Views into Your Home Checklist:

1. No ugly backsides of furnishings exposed.

2. No ugly backsides of picture frames showing.

3. Do you need shutters on the sides and back of your home?

4. Lamps. Turn them on.

5. Lamps. Use pink and white bulbs of 15, 40 and/or 60 watts mixed about.

6. Can you see the TV from the garden?

DRAWING OPPOSITE: This is a front door garden view. All of the plantings are hydrangeas. I advise my clients to be bold with the front yard.

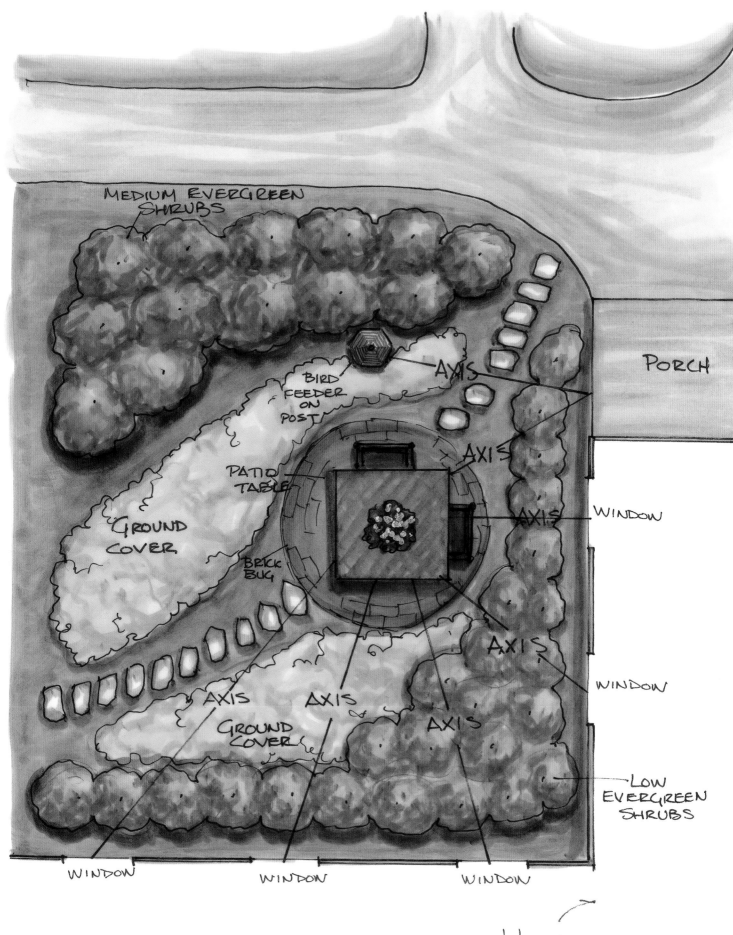

MEDIUM EVERGREEN SHRUBS

PORCH

BIRD FEEDER ON POST

AXIS

AXIS

PATIO TABLE

GROUND COVER

AXIS

WINDOW

BRICK BUG

AXIS

WINDOW

AXIS

AXIS

LOW EVERGREEN SHRUBS

GROUND COVER

WINDOW

WINDOW

WINDOW

HOUSE

Your Home is a Part of Your Garden

1. Let your home's interior and garden segue into one another.

2. Your house, exterior walls, and interior should evolve into a supporting backdrop for your garden.

3. Create areas of your garden to sit in during an evening so you can look back at your home, curtains open, lamps on. It's a refuge.

4. Effort expended in your garden will pay dividends far exceeding the effort.

5. Let go, create your garden, and enjoy the life that is waiting for you.

6. A garden about your home creates a zone of grace.

DRAWING OPPOSITE: The "L" shape of this house couldn't be clearer about where the best axes are to a focal point. Each axis has the same focal point but the different angles of view make it fresh from each location. Walk around your house, inside and outside, listening to what it tells you about where to place key axes and focal points

Necessities

Every home has them—unsightly eyesores such as air conditioning units, garbage cans, unsightly basement doors. Focal points, plantings, and deftly designed garden structures can camouflage all these home necessities.

ABOVE: Sidewalks along homes, especially with necessities of gas/electric meters, aren't a natural consideration for creating beautiful garden axes. But they should be. Whenever you have an eyesore, design a focal point nearby to create a distraction. Your camera can take a pretty garden shot from many angles. Think like your camera on a daily basis and be in complete denial about seeing necessities.

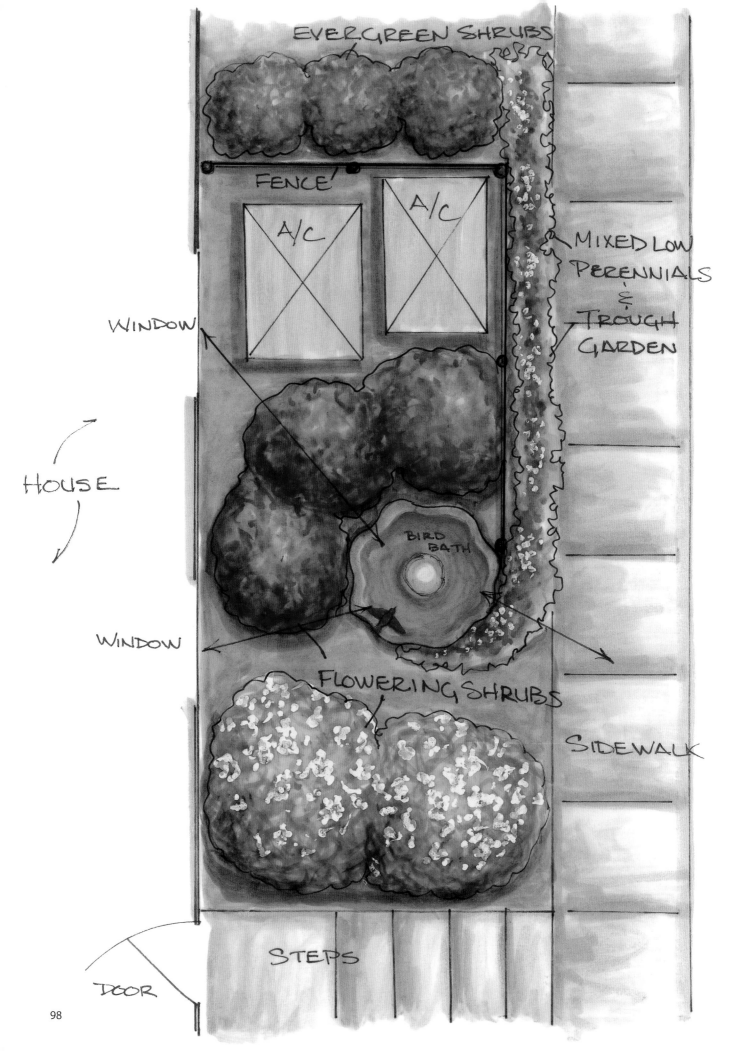

EVERGREEN SHRUBS

FENCE

A/C A/C

WINDOW

MIXED LOW
PERENNIALS
&
TROUGH
GARDEN

HOUSE

BIRD
BATH

WINDOW

FLOWERING SHRUBS

SIDEWALK

STEPS

DOOR

98

DRAWING OPPOSITE: Seen in this line drawing, the air conditioning condensers are unsightly. But as this photo shows on the previous page and the next page, they are hidden by this charming picket fence. You may always know they are there, but a garden guest and even the camera doesn't. ABOVE: With a slightly different camera angle that shown on the previous page, you can see why this garden was designed to be such a little jewel box of interest. Air-conditioners were the cause. Picket fencing further hides the eyesore with subtlety; it's painted green like the house, not white like the trim. White would draw attention to the area. You have a choice about what you want to see. Do you want to see air-conditioners or a beautiful garden?

Analyze thoroughly why a garden works aesthetically. When recreating a garden you find desirable you must understand all its elements.

TOP: Basement doors aren't known for charm. But you are looking at a path leading to a basement door that is charming. Many ingredients are involved to create this charm: urn on brick wall, nice light fixture, shutters, window box with plantings, old watering can, lush plantings near house, lots of light, good garden maintenance, downspout painted same color as house, classic urn at door. OPPOSITE: Standing at the basement door looking at the opposite axis to the picture on the opposite page. The path doesn't just go to the door, it also leads to another area of the garden; dramatized with an arbor and a pair of pots. Gardens must be easily traversed.

ABOVE: Another axis leads off the path seen in the photo on the previous page. This path runs parallel with the side of the house, a.k.a. the air-conditioning side of the house, taking you from back garden to front garden. An air-conditioning unit may be less than 10 feet away, but this sweet garden area will draw eyes away from that ugliness. RIGHT: This is the same seating area as the garden above viewed along the axis from the opposite direction—front garden to back garden. An incredible bench made of flagstone and a millstone mimics the pathway's millstone. Such detail in a small space isn't only aesthetic, it's functional—form and function. We pulled up the chairs and table to the bench and ate lunch with the gardener after finishing our photography.

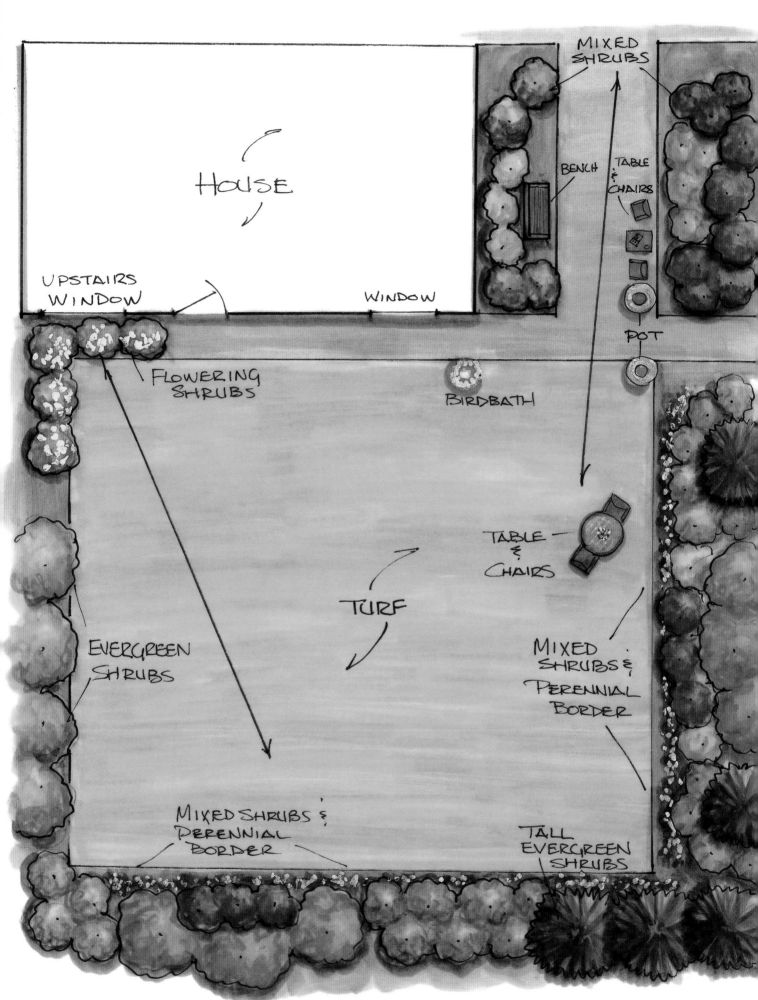

HOUSE

UPSTAIRS WINDOW

WINDOW

MIXED SHRUBS

BENCH

TABLE & CHAIRS

POT

FLOWERING SHRUBS

BIRDBATH

EVERGREEN SHRUBS

TURF

TABLE & CHAIRS

MIXED SHRUBS & PERENNIAL BORDER

MIXED SHRUBS & PERENNIAL BORDER

TALL EVERGREEN SHRUBS

"*It is the purest of human pleasures; it is the greatest refreshment to the spirits of man; without which buildings and palaces are but gross handy-works: and a man shall ever see that, when ages grow to civility and elegancy, men come to build stately sooner than to —garden finely; as if gardening were the greater perfection.*"

Sir Francis Bacon, 1625

DRAWING OPPOSITE: This garden layout looks quite simple, yet in reality, it is full of wonderful secrets. The path heightens the anticipation of what is to come at the back of the garden. Just a series of rectangles and squares are repositories of many wonders. Don't be afraid that simplicity will create a boring garden. Simplicity is often the hallmark of a good design. ABOVE: Don't fail to add wonderful places to sit in your garden. The owner of this garden and her grown children, who live within walking distance, like to have cocktails here before dinner. With classic wood furnishings, this garden is a theatrical set. Everything is movable for whatever play is performed.

Designing Beautiful Garden Views

Important Rules for Designing Beautiful Garden Views

1. Begin placement of axes with your most frequent views from the house.

2. A double axis is the view out and the view in along the same line. Each double axis should have a focal point at each end.

3. Single focal points should be a focal point of several different axes.

4. If several windows view a common location, place one focal point that can be seen from each axis.

OPPOSITE: Imagine cooking while looking at this garden view. This gardener does. She designed the area to be viewed directly from her kitchen window. Pretty from the kitchen window, it is also viewed at the entry to her large deck, from French doors in the breakfast area, and from several windows upstairs.

Important Rules for Designing Beautiful Garden Views

5. Completing axes around your home will give it a continually changing atmosphere.

6. All axes must be stunning. No axis should be left undone.

7. Your garden is important. Your environment will either support you or weaken you.

8. Double axes streamline your garden design, laying the foundation for your winter garden.

OPPOSITE: Designed for the kitchen axis, this area appears to be designed for viewing from upstairs. It will probably happen that axes you design are viewed better from different axes than you originally considered. When these types of accidents begin to happen, know that you're truly gardening. I lose all dignity when good accidents happen in my garden - "yippeeeeeeeeeeeeee."!

Important Rules for Designing Beautiful Garden Views

9. A garden designed to look good in winter will look good the rest of the year.

10. Groundcovers unite axes and focal point.

11. Having a path around your entire home creates a magic circle for "chi," life force.

12. No guilt is allowed for spending the amount of time it takes tocreate double axes.

OPPOSITE: Woodland gardens have the same garden design rules applied to them as formal gardens. Yes, this woodland bench with a section of tree trunk for a coffee table is completely designed to be on an axis. It just doesn't appear that way because of the natural setting.

Important Rules for Designing Beautiful Garden Views

13. Not completing every area of your garden immediately, will improve your garden.

14. Axes views into your home should be warm and inviting.

15. Your house, exterior walls, and interior should evolve into a supporting backdrop for your garden.

16. All focal points must be precisely level, horizontally and vertically.

17. Double axes with an enfilade are momentous.

OPPOSITE: This is a view from sitting on a woodland bench (previous page) looking at the pond and small waterfall. They are perfect double axes. It's the same design rule used formally but in a woodland setting.

ABOVE: Sitting on a garden bench, this view looks at the back of the house. A guest cottage is to the right, a potting shed to the left. For nighttime viewing, open your curtains, turn on the lamps, and enjoy the view of your home. An upstairs gable window is the view seen opposite. RIGHT: Seen from the upstairs gable window, this intriguing path forms a Dali pattern. The path, made of bricks leftover from the Atlanta, GA Olympics, was designed and installed by the homeowner, a graphic artist, to be functional and beautiful. A bench anchors the outward view of the axes.

Listen to your garden
as intensely as it listens to you.

> *You have
> a choice about
> what you want
> to see.*

RIGHT: Here's a view of the guest cottage seen from the tool shed. Leaving no axes undone created a charming entry into this guest cottage. In such a tiny backyard, this gardener knew to be dramatic at the ends of his axes.

Don't be afraid
that simplicity
will create a
boring garden.

RIGHT: This photo reveals more secrets along the Dali path. Another axis exposes a patio behind the guest cottage and a slight change in elevation. It may be just a potting shed, but its axes views are beautiful. Architect Louis Kahn would be pleased that the view from the tool shed was considered.

ABOVE: The post prematurely stops the eye but beauty is restored with the clambering vine and hanging vase of flowers. LEFT: A welcoming stone bench to sit on and a welcoming stone birdbath. Be sure to use a non-porous stone if you wish to create a bench/birdbath.

ABOVE: This is a mature garden. Gardened by the same family for over 20 years, it is a yearly discovery. Over the years, the gardeners have looked and thought: "That tree needs limbing up; The guest cottage needs a dramatic front door; A patio should be put in behind the guest cottage; I deserve a potting shed; The path should split off this way." That is what makes a beautiful garden, years of plants growing and years of refining—always refining.

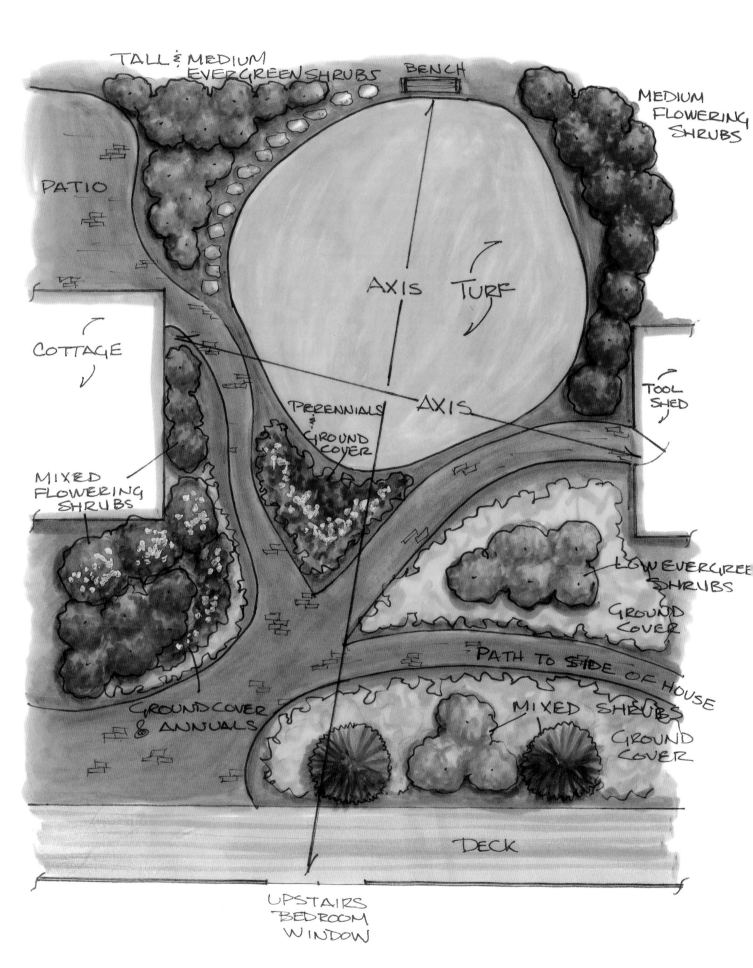

TALL & MEDIUM
EVERGREEN SHRUBS

BENCH

MEDIUM
FLOWERING
SHRUBS

PATIO

AXIS

TURF

COTTAGE

TOOL
SHED

PERENNIALS

AXIS

GROUND
COVER

MIXED
FLOWERING
SHRUBS

LOW EVERGREEN
SHRUBS

GROUND
COVER

PATH TO SIDE OF HOUSE

MIXED SHRUBS

GROUNDCOVER
& ANNUALS

GROUND
COVER

DECK

UPSTAIRS
BEDROOM
WINDOW

Whenever you have an eyesore, design a focal point nearby to create a distraction.

ABOVE: Seen from an upstairs window, this path takes on a Salvador Dali pattern. DRAWING OPPOSITE: Pathways dominate the design of this garden. Axes to the different focal points were designed to add beauty to function. If you're maintaining your own garden, it's important to design function into form.

In Closing

I've written about several different ways of creating garden axes. It may require a combination of venues—lectures, tours, classes, articles, gardening—for you to learn about axes. Some things you learn may scare you. Good. I do mean to knock you out of your comfort zone. As a beginning gardener, only plants were allowed in my garden—off with your head if you hinted that I needed focal points or that they be placed according to some template with crazy things called axes. A garden will change that kind of attitude.

Placing axes is easy for me now—not instant, but easy. This book describes almost 100 guidelines for axes. Guidelines place axes for me; that's why it's easy.

ABOVE: Good garden accidents will occur in your garden if you keep learning and refining. Pictured left and right are two views of the same axes with enfilades. It was designed beautifully with a master's touch, but the angle of the views you are looking at were never considered by the designer. These are the types of good garden accidents you will experience when all the elements of garden design"color, line, texture, form, axes, enfilades, and more—are ingredients of your garden. Design with the rules, break them when you are passionate, and do expect serendipitous beauty to arrive - more than you designed.
DRAWING OPPOSITE: A gardener bought this home with all the hardscapes already in place but no garden. She looked for important axes and created focal point views there, while amplifying them by making them enfilades—a view through to a view. This drawing is of the pool and statue seen in right photo above.

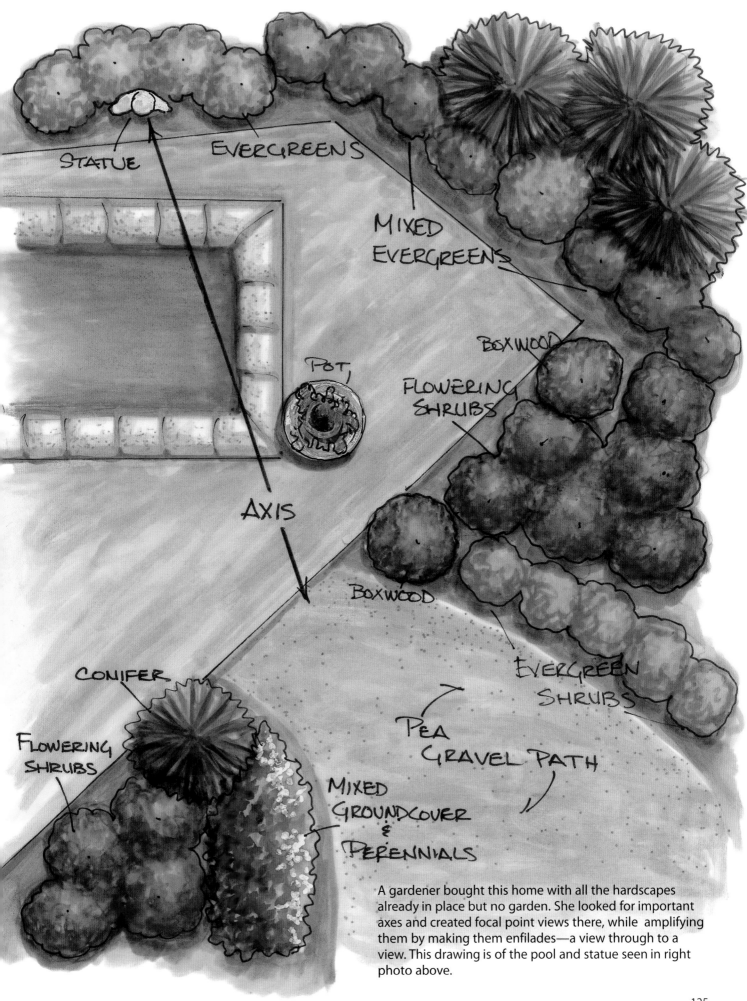

STATUE

EVERGREENS

MIXED
EVERGREENS

POT

BOXWOOD

FLOWERING
SHRUBS

AXIS

BOXWOOD

EVERGREEN
SHRUBS

CONIFER

PEA
GRAVEL PATH

FLOWERING
SHRUBS

MIXED
GROUNDCOVER
&
PERENNIALS

A gardener bought this home with all the hardscapes already in place but no garden. She looked for important axes and created focal point views there, while amplifying them by making them enfilades—a view through to a view. This drawing is of the pool and statue seen in right photo above.

A

Accessorize 85
Annual/s 20,58
Arbor 44, 52, 72, 74
Architecture 9, 17, 56
Aristotle 10
Art 35, 36, 38, 41, 43, 44, 49, 58, 99
Axis/es 9, 11, 16, 24, 28, 30, 35, 38, 44, 49, 52, 54, 68, 71, 77, 78, 81, 85, 89, 93, 106, 109, 111, 112

B

Backdrop 11, 50, 89, 95, 112
Backyard 11, 50, 116
Bacon, Sir Francis 105
Bench/es 10, 11, 13, 16, 19, 28, 31, 56, 61, 72, 110, 114
Bird/s/feeder 38, 43, 49, 58, 89
Bloom/s 33, 89
Bond house & garden 86
Bourgeois 35, 36, 66
Boxwood/s 49, 56, 64, 68, 72
Bridge 32, 35, 38
Budget 35, 36, 66

C

Camera 96, 97, 98
Canopy 13, 58
Catbird seat 83
Chair/s 67, 72, 89
Chi 44, 110
Children 40, 44, 99, 105
Classic 26, 33, 36, 38, 100, 102, 105
Cluster Mansion/s 36
Color 9, 20, 32, 84, 100, 124
Conscious aesthetic 36
Copy 50, 58, 124
Creativity 35

D - E

Dali, Salvador 115, 118, 123, 127
Deleot, Katharine 41
Design/ed/s 9, 26, 33, 41, 47, 49, 50, 52, 54, 56, 58, 59, 62, 63, 65, 67, 68, 69, 70, 72, 77, 78, 80, 86, 89, 97, 99, 105, 106, 107, 109, 110, 111, 112, 121, 123, 124
Dormant 67
Double Axis 9, 19, 26, 72, 106,
Drama 33, 89
Drift/s 58
Einstein, Albert 55, 65

Enfilade 26, 72, 112, 124, 127
Entryway/s 36, 41, 49, 50, 81
Epiphany/ies 7, 11, 72, 86
Estate sale 33, 36
Evergreen/s 19, 33, 48, 49, 50, 52, 55, 74
Exit/s 49, 50
Eyesore 96, 97, 99, 123

F

Fence 9, 26, 41, 52, 53, 98
Feng shui 41, 127
Focal point/s 9, 13, 16, 19, 24, 26, 31, 33, 34, 35, 36, 38, 55, 56, 62, 65, 68, 71, 72, 77, 78, 83, 95, 96, 97, 106, 110, 112, 121, 123, 125
Foliage 40, 79
Form 4, 32, 36, 104, 124
Formal 33, 38, 43, 44, 47, 60, 62, 86, 110
Front yard 67, 93
Function/al 64, 91, 102, 115, 123

G

Garbage cans 26, 31, 65, 94
Garden/s 9, 11, 13, 15, 16, 19, 24, 26, 28, 30, 38, 41, 43, 44, 48, 50, 52, 53, 54, 56, 58, 61, 62, 63, 65, 67, 68, 71, 72, 74, 76, 77, 78, 81, 83, 85, 86, 86, 90, 91, 92, 97, 99, 100, 102, 106, 108, 109, 111, 112, 114, 118, 121, 123, 125
Garden design 9, 11, 19, 26, 34, 40, 49, 52, 58, 62, 67, 68, 76, 109, 111, 124
Garden room/s 9, 33, 38, 48, 89, 71
Gardenese 68, 127
Gate 41, 44, 47, 52, 55
Grace 68, 95

H - I - J

Hardscape 33, 36
Hydrangea/s 50, 56, 58, 75, 85, 93
Hedge 26, 34, 85
Illusion 13, 52, 55
Informal 40, 46, 57
Interior/s 11, 13, 19, 77, 81, 86, 89, 94, 112
Intuitive 9
Joy 26, 68
Jung, Carl 35

K - L

Kadinsky, Der Blaue Reiter 41

Kahn, Louis 118
Koan 9, 127
Lamp/s 86, 89, 93, 95
Lawn 19, 26, 38, 41, 44
Line/s 10, 15, 31, 35, 43, 44, 50, 60, 62, 98, 124
Lush 26, 72, 79, 89, 100
Luther, Martin 26

M - N - O

Magic/al 38, 41, 44, 68, 111
Maintenance 9, 11
Mission statement 33
Money 9, 33, 36
More impact, less imput 9, 33
Morpheus 89
Native 43, 44, 47
Organic living 11

P

Parterre 20, 23
Path/s/way 8, 9, 16, 33, 38, 39, 40, 41, 43, 44, 47, 52, 55, 61, 68, 71, 72, 74, 82, 100, 102, 103, 105, 111, 115, 118 120, 122, 123
Patio 41, 105, 118, 121
Pattern/s 20, 49, 52, 115, 123
Perennials 15, 67, 72, 127
Picasso 38
Planters/pots 37
Plinth/s 8, 9, 33, 36, 89
Pond 11, 24, 26, 28, 36, 38, 72, 112
Pool 41, 124
Potting shed 114, 118, 121
Pugin, A.W.N. 9

Q - R

Quality 32, 36, 86
Refine/ing 65, 121, 124
Refuge 88, 94
Repetition 68, 71
Rescue/d 35, 36

S

Sackville-West, Vita 8
Scale 35, 36, 47, 54
Scott, Sir Walter 11
Serendipity 38
Serenity 20, 68, 83
Shrub/s 11, 13, 15, 44, 48, 50, 52, 58, 72
Shutters 19, 85, 93
Silhouettes 49, 52, 74

Sissinghurst 9
Site 33, 89
Snow/ed 48, 50, 52
Spring 61
Strong, Sir Roy 81
Structure 49, 50, 52, 54, 62, 86, 90
Style 11, 13, 15, 23, 33, 36, 38, 56, 81, 85
Summer 50, 67
Surprise/s 19, 35, 36, 38

T

Table/s 37, 41, 67, 72, 84, 86, 89, 102, 110
Tapestry 38
Terminus 9,32
Texture 50, 54, 124
Theory into practice 30
Time 10, 16, 26, 33, 36, 56, 58, 59, 61, 62, 66, 70, 72, 75, 78, 79, 111
Tools 64
Tour/ing/s 8, 41, 60, 62, 64, 124
Tree/s 13, 19, 31, 32, 38, 41, 49, 46, 50, 52, 58, 67, 72, 74, 81, 86, 96, 110, 120

U - V

Ubiquitous 26, 31
Understory 13, 58
Urn/s 33, 36, 72, 81, 100
View/ing/s 9, 11, 16, 18, 19, 20, 24, 26, 28, 30, 37, 38, 39, 41, 44, 45, 53, 56, 58, 61, 62, 65, 67, 71, 72, 74, 76, 77, 78, 83, 85, 86, 87, 89, 93, 95, 106. 109. 112. 114, 115, 116, 124
Vine/s 12, 33, 52, 72

W

Wall/s 48, 52, 89, 95, 100, 112
Water 86
Weeping 33, 36, 50
Wheeler, Candice 90
Window/s 11, 14, 19, 20, 23, 26, 31, 36, 41, 56, 72, 78, 84, 86, 88, 100, 106, 114, 123
Winter 48, 49, 50, 52, 55, 61, 67, 74, 109, 111
Woodland 38, 43, 49, 90, 100, 112

X Y Z

Zone 58, 68, 95, 124

Inches to Millimeters and Centimeters

Inches	MM	CM
1/8	3	.3
1/4	6	.6
3/8	10	1.0
1/2	13	1.3
5/8	16	1.6
3/4	19	1.9
7/8	22	2.2
1	25	2.5
1-1/4	32	3.2
1-1/2	38	3.8
1-3/4	44	4.4
2	51	5.1
3	76	7.6
4	102	10.2
5	127	12.7
6	152	15.2
7	178	17.8
8	203	20.3
9	229	22.9
10	254	25.4
11	279	27.9
12	305	30.5

Yards to Meters

Yards	Meters
1/8	.11
1/4	.23
3/8	.34
1/2	.46
5/8	.57
3/4	.69
7/8	.80
1	.91
2	1.83
3	2.74
4	3.66
5	4.57
6	5.49
7	6.40
8	7.32
9	8.23
10	9.14

COMMONLY USED TERMS

ANNUALS - plants that flower and die at the end of their season

AXES - in a garden are views along a line.

DALI-SALVADOR - exponent of Surrealism

DOUBLE AXES - as used by TD—a single axis line with a focal point at each end

ENFILADE - a view through to a view

EVERGREEN - plants that remain green all year

FENG SHUI - Chinese art of placement

FOCAL POINT - a hardscape object like a statue or a stunning plant like a maple tree in fall

GARDENESE - language of beauty, joy, serenity and grace

KOAN - epiphany

PARTERRE - garden beds in a pattern separated by paths

PERENNIALS - plants that flower and live for years